NONVERBAL COMMUNICATION

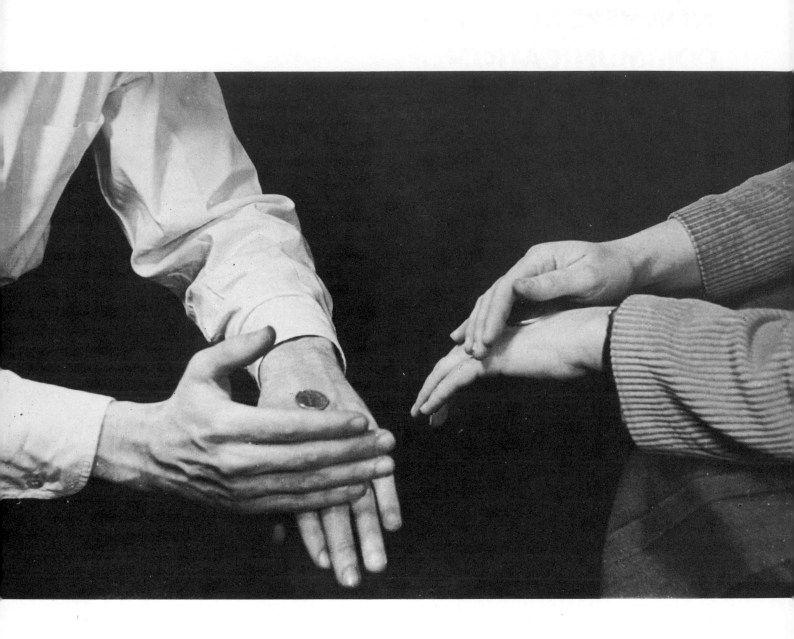

NONVERBAL COMMUNICATION

NOTES ON THE VISUAL PERCEPTION OF HUMAN RELATIONS

BY JURGEN RUESCH
and WELDON KEES

University of California Press
Berkeley, Los Angeles, London

University of California Press
Berkeley and Los Angeles
University of California Press, Ltd.
London, England
Copyright, 1956
by The Regents of the University of California
First Paperback Edition, 1972
Second Printing, 1974
ISBN: 0-520-02162-2
Library of Congress Catalog Card Number: 55-11228
Manufactured in the United States of America
Designed by Rita Carroll

FOREWORD

The study of the communicative behavior of man can be traced back to the advent of historical records and the discovery of archaeological evidence. Not until recently, however, was the study of communication systematically undertaken, thus extending a trend initiated by early scribes, priests, humanists, and artists. Numerous contributions from the fields of linguistics, anthropology, sociology, psychiatry, psychoanalysis, semantics, mathematics, cybernetics, and neurophysiology have greatly broadened our knowledge of human communication. However, the theoretical and systematic study of communication has serious limitations, inasmuch as scientific thinking and reporting are dependent upon verbal and digital language systems whereas human interaction, in contrast, is much more related to nonverbal systems of codification. Although most people are familiar with the rules that govern verbal communication—logic, syntax, and grammar—few are aware of the principles that apply to nonverbal communication.

This book is the result of an attempt to penetrate this more or less unexplored territory. We have attempted to investigate a number of the nonverbal ways in which people communicate with each other. With the aid of still photography, we have tried to explore the informal and often spontaneous methods of communication that, when considered in verbal and, particularly, in abstract terms, tend grossly to distort actual events. Being well aware of the fact that photography introduces still another kind of distortion, we consider the present book only as a first and rough introduction to the subject of nonverbal communication. It is our hope that, with the use of nonverbal denotation devices, and with a fuller understanding of the problems of nonverbal communication, better ways may be found to approach a number of difficulties encountered in human relations, education, and mental health.

The work upon which this book is based was done in the Division of Psychiatry of the University of California School of Medicine and the Langley Porter Clinic, San Francisco, and was supported in part by a grant from the National Institute of Mental Health, United States Public Health Service.

Without the help of a number of persons, some of our problems would have been far more troublesome. We are particularly grateful to Gregory Bateson for his always intelligent criticism and for a number of his photographs, which we used in the third section of this book. The photographs of the interiors of houses are included through the kind coöperation of six families who, for the sake of this research, were good enough to tolerate the authors and their cameras. Although these families must remain anonymous, it is only because of their forbearance and patience that this work has been made possible. Dr. Lillian Bennett was invaluable for her help in studying and commenting upon the pictures of private homes and interiors. We owe a very considerable debt to Ann Kees, who read the manuscript and made innumerable helpful suggestions, and to Susan West, who assisted in the preparation of the manuscript and in various other ways.

The difficulties involved in procuring certain photographs were solved for us through the very kind assistance of a number of individuals. Dr. Robert Wartenberg and the Year Book Publishers, Inc., granted permission for the reproduction of the four photographs on Plate 78. Herbert Cahoon, now of the Morgan Library, was of great help in locating, in the New York Public Library, the pictures we have used in Plate 3. We thank the *San Francisco Chronicle,* and particularly Alfred Frankenstein and Madeleine O'Connor, for a photograph that is reproduced in Plate 22. To Dr. Jermayne MacAgy, Robert Greensfelder, and Barbara and Frank Stauffacher, we are grateful for certain suggestions.

San Francisco   J. R.

                                                                                                                     W. K.

CONTENTS

ILLUSTRATIONS

1 THE FRAME OF REFERENCE

The word *communication* will be used here in a very broad sense to include all of the procedures by which one mind may affect another. This, of course, involves not only written and oral speech, but also music, the pictorial arts, the theatre, the ballet, and in fact all human behavior.

Warren W. Weaver

1. MODERN THEORIES AND METHODS

We must assume that people have communicated with each other in some way since mankind has existed, and that they handed down from generation to generation the methods of communication that developed over the course of centuries. For thousands of years an elite held a monopoly on written communication. As the humanities and the arts gradually became a part of the curriculum of higher education, knowledge about communication and training in communicative methods were made accessible to large numbers of the population.

The Contemporary Scene

Today the American social scene literally buzzes with people who are directly or indirectly concerned with the facilitation and improvement of communication. Indeed, one of the **outstanding characteristics of our time is** a deep and pervasive **concern with communication** (127). In medicine, for example, the doctor-patient relationship has recently been given studious attention; the problems of labor-management relations in industry seem continual; retailers, wholesalers, and businessmen worry about public relations. And along with the growing solicitude that prevails in almost every walk of life concerning such interconnections, however fragmented they may actually be, has gone the development of communication machinery and institutions—in particular, the radio, television, movies, and the press (151). In these fields, along with others employing thousands of workers in the sciences, popular arts, and applied communications, an army of specialists is engaged in receiving, evaluating, and transmitting information.

But such developments are not without dangers, and the nightmarish dreams of the future depicted by Aldous Huxley in *Brave New World* (70) and George Orwell in *Nineteen Eighty-four* (115) seem to be almost upon us. For example, the specialists in **mass communication,** recruited largely from radio and television, advertising, propaganda, and the big circulation magazines, seem to gear their operations to a single end: capturing an audience and controlling its thought. Often the advertisers (20) share with the popularizers the intent to shape a world in which the principle of least effort is supposed to pay off: a world in which everyone will smile without letup and where every problem has a solution, where every ache and worry—even loneliness and despair—can be speedily and painlessly dispelled. The advertisers project the idea that despair may be hidden and loneliness may wear a mask; actually a contorted smile may be more alarming than a sober expression of preoccupation, and an assumed gaiety more distressing than an honest statement of disappointment.

The **commercialization** of mass communication has led to a depersonalization of human relations and to a glorification of clichés and slogans. The standardized response begins more and more to substitute for deeply felt, personalized expression, and—as a perhaps last defense—the human ear has adapted itself to sort and disregard a considerable number of verbal messages that emerge from radio loudspeakers and television sets, just as it formerly accommodated itself to the task of absorbing what was being said. This trend goes even further. As mass communication increasingly tends toward sloganizing and the use of proven formulas, literature tends toward journalism, reversing a trend of two hundred years during which journalism aspired to the condition of literature. Many book publishers frankly admit that they have become less and less adventurous and chance taking in matters of editorial policy, looking most searchingly for best sellers to relax the economic squeeze in which they are caught, or relying on instructional and inspirational "how to do it" books, in which everything is reduced to a recipe or device that is simple and can be quickly acquired by everyone. When the "how to" is violently disjoined from the "what"—one of the major trends of popular thinking today—communication is regarded as merely a peripheral skill unrelated to the core of personality and to all those thoughts and feelings that formerly characterized an individual human being.

This trend is also responsible for shaping hollow and unreal face-to-face encounters that in even the recent past would have been considered not only unethical but definitely pathological. Today's salesmen, for example, are trained to turn on a line, to envisage for the customer a sense of prestige and success that attends the purchase of an expensive car that the customer may not be able to afford, or to create feelings of emergency and fear when grooming and personal hygiene are involved. The line between fantasy and reality becomes increasingly blurred, and the individual is given less and less of a chance to live in an environment where honest and well-meant advice is obtainable. The upsurge of psychiatric treatment is thus not unrelated to these developments, as more and more people have come to feel that they are lost in an unreal world and want to find themselves.

Present-day thinking has created a **verbal unreality**. Primarily in middle-class circles—particularly among many administrators, executives, almost all politicians, and even doctors and lawyers—words tend to be treated as absolutes. The fact that words are sounds referring to ideas or events is frequently overlooked altogether; in the act of speaking or writing, words are invested, in their minds, with substance and body, so that words become things in themselves. Then too, the assumption is often made that words are the only means of communication, whereas commonplace silent actions are not interpreted as having communicative value.

The Machiavellian use of communication for deception and control has been employed for centuries, but the commercialization of communication in business and politics is a fairly recent development. These new techniques not only employ deception about products—a device merchants have always worked—but have introduced a radically new idea: to delude the individual about his own personal attitudes toward other people and things. This approach in effect undermines his ethical and moral sense, and destroys his trust in his fellow men. Against these recent developments, few defensive measures have yet developed. However, a **countertrend** is apparent. As educators and religious and civic leaders have become alarmed at the trend of events, a growing intellectual and scientific consciousness about communication as a problem has developed. In certain literary circles, among those who deal with language and semantics—and increasingly among some psychiatrists—there is a deepening regard for problems of meaning and a concern with the individualistic and idiosyncratic attributes of words as opposed to their dictionary definitions. Cybernetics engineers and biologists have dealt with the communication networks and feedback patterns; psychiatrists, cultural anthropologists, and social workers have studied problems of social action and interpersonal and group relations.

The trend of a number of these approaches has been toward an essential **concern with nonverbal forms of communication** and with the verbal form largely in its pragmatic aspects. Such a reaction against the overevaluation of the spoken and printed word, and against both commercialism and the relative exclusion of nonverbal elements, can in one sense be interpreted as a move toward safety. In a time of political or ideological crisis, there exists a tendency to censor words in the naïve belief that thought can be brought under absolute control. Although books can be burned, the use of certain words legally outlawed, and even the act of listening to particular broadcasts or speeches marked as a criminal offense, communication through silent action is more difficult to suppress. It has been widely noted how, under authoritarian regimes, human beings turn more and more toward the perception of the nonverbal, the evaluation of nonverbally codified things, and expression through gesture and action.

The present book was written in the midst of such contemporary trends in communication. We are well aware that much of the material and many of the ideas are far from new. Some of them are basic to the fields of science and medicine; some derive from the work of artists, novelists, poets, actors, and movie makers; some of them, indeed, are commonplace to everyone, though they are rarely expressed in verbal terms. In venturing beyond our own respective fields, we are probably open to criticism. The material may appear to some too simple and self-evident, and to others too all-encompassing or abstract. But in a society such as ours, with its emphasis on narrowing skills, interests, and ideas, the attempt to integrate some of the notions pertaining to human relations around the theory of communication can be justified as at least an attempt to escape the limiting, the specialized, and the fragmented.

Theoretical Considerations

Communicative behavior is usually observed in four different settings, characterized by differences in magnitude of the **system**: (127)

> The intrapersonal or intrapsychic communication system is self-contained within one person. The places of origin and destination of messages are within the same organism, and the principal functions are commonly referred to as "thinking" and "feeling."
>
> The interpersonal system comprises communication between two persons.
>
> The group system embraces several or many persons known to one another, all of whom occupy specialized positions within the network of the group.
>
> The societal system includes so many persons that individuals can be considered only statistically; the individual's identity is lost; and communication is considered an interaction of groups or large bodies of persons.

The human **functions of communication** serve the purpose of mediating information across the boundary lines of the human organism or the group organization. Specifically, they solve the problem of how events outside an organism or an organization are represented in terms of information on the inside, and how events on the inside are relayed to the outside. The functions of communication include:

Perception—that is, the reception of incoming signals

Evaluation, which also involves memory and the retention of past experiences as well as decision making

Transmission and expression of information

For our present purposes we shall be concerned primarily with the processes of perception and transmission, and among the processes of perception with **visual perception** in particular (13). The human eye is an unparalleled distance receiver, but effective visual perception is relatively late in developing. The child's exploration begins with its immediate environment and moves gradually to more distant objects. Only at the age of five or six do children begin to perceive with some spontaneity such remotely situated objects as airplanes, birds in flight, or ships on the horizon. Not only are the eyes distance receivers, but the number of objects and persons encompassed at a single glance is large. Unlike our hands, which, equipped with the end organs of touch, can explore only a few things at any one time, the act of scanning the horizon creates a situation in which the observer often needs to decide which particular object or person within range should be focused upon or regarded at greater length. Of particular relevance here is the concept of cue, which may be defined as a perception having problem-solving properties. For example, some of the cues in the perception of space are (57) the relative size of objects, the interposition of objects in front of each other, linear perspective of convergent or divergent lines, the presence or absence of texture such as occurs in aerial views, differences in light and shade, as well as those cues related to stereoscopic vision and ocular convergence sensations. Movement in space is perceived by the eye with the help of differences in angular velocity between the fixated moving object and other stationary objects. Both apparent movement—stimuli appearing at intervals in different places but arising from stationary objects—and real movement of actual objects are assessed by such cues as the length of pause between stimuli, duration of exposure, distance between stimuli, and color differences.

Or so perception psychology has it. In terms of communication, however, perception is treated along with evaluation and transmission as components of a single unit. In **social action,** for example, the self is always proprioceptively as well as exteroceptively perceived as part of the situation. Perception in such terms is inseparable from evaluation. Movement is not conceived as proceeding from one point in space to another point—or simply from A to B; the self is additionally considered as a triangulation point. Movement is then assessed as toward or away from the self, or the self on a line of action or away from it. Similarly, distance is not judged in terms of specific physical measurement, but also in terms of biological implications—for example, whether a goal is within walking or reaching distance. In the assessment of social actions, therefore, one or more persons comprise the permanent points of orientation, and events are dealt with not only in terms of their physical characteristics but also in terms of their human origins and impact. Considerations of such an approach illuminate a striking difference between the cultural anthropologist and the novelist on the one hand and the physicist and the sociologist on the other. The former observe, interpret, and act upon events with the human being as the central and permanent frame of reference. The latter treat the individual human being either as an organism made up of molecules or as an anonymous particle in large social structures.

For the communication specialist, the individual still has an identity, and all kinds of information may have relevance; consequently he is primarily interested in the symbolic and referential properties of events. When a person observes a series of events and then wishes to make a statement about them, such a statement has to be represented by signs that are comprehensible to others. The technical aspects of this process are referred to as **codification**. In human interaction the most frequent codification systems are: personal appearance and dress; gestures; such ordinary actions as those connected with eating and drinking; traces of activity such as footprints and material objects; and simple sounds, spoken words, and written words. Thus any action or thing may have symbolic properties and represent some other event. Knowledge and information enable the human being to reconstruct past events, understand present events, and to predict and anticipate those of the future.

When communicating with each other, people not only exchange messages containing information that refers to outside events, but they also exchange messages referring to the communication process itself. These **metacommunicative messages** include:

The specific instructions given by a sender about the way messages ought to be interpreted and the respective interpretations made by the receiver

Implicit instructions contained in what is commonly referred to as role

Institutionalized instructions, either explicit or implicit, that are inherent in the structure of social situations and the rules governing the flow of messages

When a person has expressed an idea in words to others, a reaction is necessarily expected. And this reaction contributes to clarify, extend, or alter the original idea. **Feedback**, therefore, refers to the process of correction through incorporation of information about effects achieved. When a person perceives the results produced by his own actions, the information so derived will influence subsequent actions. Feedback of information thus becomes a steering device upon which learning and the correction of errors and misunderstandings are based (163, 164).

In short, people communicate by making statements (128). These statements are signals that are coded in various prearranged ways. When they impinge upon earlier impressions, they become signs. These signs, in the strictest sense of the word, exist only in the minds of people, because their interpretation is based upon prior agreements. A statement becomes a message when it has been perceived and interpreted by another person. Finally, when sender and receiver can consensually validate an interpretation, then communication has been sucessful.

Since this book is concerned with messages codified in nonverbal terms, a word needs to be said about codifications that qualify as **language**. The definition of the term "language" is based upon a number of different criteria. According to Morris (105), language is composed of a plurality of signs, the significance of which must be known to a number of interpreters. Furthermore, these signs must be of such a nature that they can be produced by human beings and will retain the same significance in different situations. Finally, in order to enter into a variety of complex language processes, such signs must be set into patterns that are agreed upon.

The requirement that a sign be interpersonal in order to qualify as a language, however, is not incompatible with individual variations of interpretation. Variations in understanding are not necessarily due to a failure of the signifying function of a sign but to the fact that ideas remain unexpressed. In daily life human beings are rarely able to do more than to hint at what they desire to express, inasmuch as the very nature of their needs often forces them to exchange messages without delay in time. Thus it is left to the receiver to fill in unexpressed details. But whereas discrepancies in interpretation of detail are permissible as long as signs remain interpersonal, they cease to qualify as language symbols if their significance is known to only one person.

Recent development shed new light on the differences between two ways of codifying information. One of these, **analogic codification**, constitutes a series of symbols that in their proportions and relations are similar to the thing, idea, or event for which they stand. For example, railroad systems have small-scale models of their rail networks, including such details as stations, tunnels, and tracks situated along bas-relief models of the terrain. A model like this may be viewed as being analogous to the actual railroad system itself. Such a form of codification deals with continuous functions, unlike **digital codification**, which deals with discrete step intervals. The two foremost examples of digital codification are the numerical system and the phonetic alphabet. No gradual transition exists between any one letter of the alphabet and the next, or between any one number in the numerical system and the next. Information transmitted through such a system is obviously coded through various combinations of letters or digits.

The differences between these two ways of codifying information became a highly determinative factor in the construction of modern **computers** and giant brains. Many industrial machines have control devices embodying a physical analogy to the functions requiring regulation. The structure of these control devices remains relatively simple if the task is not too complex. But when the problem of control is an involved one, a digital type of machine has proved to be more versatile and adaptable to diversified problems. In such a machine the data of the problems to be controlled are presented in terms of numbers, and are then processed in accordance with the rules of arithmetic or any other kind of formal logic (123).

The **principles of analogic codification as contrasted with digital codification** have a central importance to students of human behavior that is still perhaps insufficiently understood. The use of words, whether in speech or in writing, has certain limitations akin to those of the digital computers: words remain identifying or typifying symbols that usually lack the impelling immediacy of analogic devices. Words or a series of words are emergent phenomena that, because of their step characteristics, lack the property of efficiently representing continua or changes over time. The fist of a prize fighter moves within a fraction of a second to strike the opponent's chin, but a considerably longer period of time is necessary to report such an event verbally. However, the idea of a moment in a prizefight can be quickly indicated by reënactment through gesture in approximately the same time sequence as the original event. Nonverbal communication obviously utilizes analogic codification devices. Thus various kinds of actions, pictures, or material objects represent analogic types of denotation.

In terms of codification, "digital" contrasts with "analogic"; in language terms, "discursive" contrasts with "nondiscursive." One of the capacities that distinguish man from animals is his ability to relate with others through the use of **discursive language** and to agree or disagree (26). Discursive language depends upon logic, made up of a set of artificial rules that have been agreed upon, expressed in verbal terms about a circumscribed kind of work. Logic dispenses with analogic codifications altogether, in spite of the fact that most of our thinking and communication is dependent upon the nonverbal as well as the verbal. If logic has any usefulness—and obviously it does—then a system comparable to logic would seem to be needed for coping with analogic codifications. So far, to our knowledge, this has not been seriously studied. Benjamin Lee Whorf said: "We cut nature up, organize it into concepts, and ascribe significances as we do, largely because we are parties to an agreement to organize it in this way—an agreement that holds throughout our speech community and is codified in the patterns of our language" (162).

Exposure to a particular kind of climate, culture, and to particular social situations is responsible for the development of widely differing views and individual attitudes. These become reflected in **imagery**, and lead to the development of a verbal language that attempts to correspond with, and to express, these experiences. For example, Eskimos are almost continuously exposed to snow. Consequently they have developed several concepts of snow—falling snow, snow on the ground, snow packed hard like ice, slushy snow, and wind-driven, flying snow. In our own language the concept of snow is expressed by one word—an inclusive term that would be unthinkable to the Eskimo (162).

Western thought, including scientific logic, has been largely based—or was until recently—upon an Aristotelian approach, which in turn is rooted in the Greek grammar and its **subject-predicate language structure**. Within such a structure the subject of discourse has to be stated and the level of abstraction defined. This is not true, for example, in Chinese logic and language in which the subject-predicate dichotomy is avoided(27). It is not without interest that the tremendous advances made in Western technology developed only when scientists adopted a language that was not bound by the subject-predicate dichotomy—namely, mathematics. Agreement should not be confused, however, with understanding. People shaking hands, for example, are responding to each other and carrying out complementary actions, although internally they may disagree on the significance or sincerity of this action. Consequently, nonverbal analogic codifications can be employed only for purposes of mutual understanding and complementation of action rather for purposes of agreement (129).

This fact, however, does not eliminate analogic codifications from the process of communication; it merely assigns a different position to them. If words are to be used significantly, they must still evoke pictorial images in the mind of a reader or listener (23) (30) (114). The writer depends, necessarily, upon evoking nonverbal images through verbal means, and it is precisely these nonverbal images that make possible emotional expression through words. For example, the problem of the poet, who deals with nonverbal experiences in verbal terms, is accentuated by T. S. Eliot's theory of the **"objective correlative,"** in which he holds that only through the use of words that evoke exact and striking images can an emotional response be produced in the reader. A poem, in Eliot's view, is not the "expression of personal emotion," for "the only way of expressing emotion in the form of art is by finding an 'objective correlative'; in other words, a set of objects, a situation, a chain of events which shall be the formula of that particular emotion; such that when the external facts, which must terminate in sensory experience, are given, the emotion is immediately evoked" (37). In speech it is not always necessary to evoke images, since the things to which the words refer may be close at hand and perceptible. When a man talks about his dog for example, and the dog is lying at his feet, the words used about the dog are complemented and reinforced by the animal's presence (61) (62).

The failure to distinguish between two basic principles, with their specific characteristics, has created widespread confusion, particularly in fields where accurate observation of events is held to be basic. When a **psychiatrist** wishes to report information about human behavior, he is obviously faced with a dilemma. To use words—that is, digital codification—to report what his patient says entails a minimum of distortion, and the psychiatrist is known to prefer to talk about the verbal behavior of patients rather than about their nonverbal actions. But when he uses words to talk about nonverbal behavior, complications arise. Occasionally such difficulties are solved by interposing some kind of analogic scheme between verbal reporting and the actual observation of behavior. For example, the terms "oral" and "anal" are used to evoke analogic associations in the mind of the listener about certain relations dealing with the passage of material and information through boundary openings. Thus words may be used to appeal to analogic thinking. Then too, it is obvious that analogic types of codification are of the greatest value in suggesting the quality of the continuous and the immediacy of impact implicit in the actual visual world.

In most present-day cultures, marked as they are by **culture contact,** many individuals are involved in events that run contrary to the experiences of the majority. Then such individuals tend to cluster in groups and to develop their own language; under such circumstances the verbal language is more or less shared with other groups, whereas the nonverbal language appears to be more particularistic. However, there exist people for whom even this solution is inaccessible. Although artists tend to cluster in groups or at least tend to have a sense of shared relationship in terms of such codifications, the mentally sick, whose verbal difficulties are known, differ from such groups as artists in being incapable of using even analogic codifications for purposes of communication. Through unfavorable childhood experiences these people failed to learn communication successfully and to share certain ways of denotation with others; as a result they became lonely, deviant, and marginal. Such peripheral individuals are usually incapable of expressing their thoughts and emotions verbally, and consequently of reaching agreements with others. However, some are highly sophisticated in terms of analogic thinking and expression. Such persons stand out in a markedly deviant way when, in our digitally oriented schools, they fail to live up to the standards set for reading, writing, and arithmetic, although they may be talented in athletics, dancing, craftsmanship, music, or painting.

Photography and the Recording of Visually Perceived Events

Until the advent of photography, engraving, drawing, painting, and sculpture were the principal means by which people recorded their visual impressions. Literal representation was rarely a problem. Indeed, it was only during the brief span of history from the Renaissance to the beginnings of impressionism that the "realistic" portrayal of objects, employing linear and aerial perspective, modeling, and "true" light and color, was held to be a matter of central concern. At no point in the history of art was painting or sculpture "photographic." Even those artists who proclaimed allegiance to the "literal" and the "real" shaped nature out of some personal vision and individual sense of order, emphasizing one thing more than another. Thus it was not until 1839, when Daguerre introduced nitric acid and a copper plate to a camera obscura, that it at last became possible, in a variant of Lumière's phrase, to "open a window on the world." The way then lay open to record nature frankly, naturalistically, and at first hand, and to pin down its enormous and proliferating detail with speed, ease, and a high degree of accuracy.

The early masters of the camera, such as Brady, Hill, Atget, Stieglitz (110), among others, were quick to grasp the potentialities of a medium that could handle everyday life—a medium, in Clement Greenberg's words, "clean of past and tradition, through which they could sense contemporary reality naively and express it directly, untrammeled by reminiscences and precedents" (58). Such twentieth-century disciples of "straight" **photography** as Walker Evans (40) and Berenice Abbott (97) bore down even more heavily on exploiting the commonplace, evolving an approach, particularly in Evans' case, that was spare, rigorous, and clinical.

With the further development of camera techniques, scientists, press photographers, and others began shooting **candid, unstaged, naturalistic events** in order to catch every aspect of human and animal life (16). For the first time in history such permanent visual records enabled people not only to document events but also to disseminate information and to spread news nonverbally from one place to another and from generation to generation. Until very recent times the cumulative body of information was dependent upon spoken or written accounts; but today the "canning and preserving" of events makes it possible for nonparticipants to witness current and past events at almost any time and any place. The photographic document has assumed the position of a codification system, and indeed has approximated an external visual model of the world (53). Thus the visual and auditory recording of historical events will perhaps make it possible to retain progressively more of the nonverbal elements influencing both the trivial and the world-shaking decisions that are made every day and that, because they are based on nonverbal cues, often escape our attention..

Although photography is unable to reproduce the manner in which people actually evaluate their visual perceptions, it at least records the events that the eye *might* have perceived. But photographers were not satisfied with these limitations; instead, they were always striving toward a method that would enable them to reconstruct more closely what the eye actually perceives. The invention and subsequent perfection of **movie photography** satisfied these wishes beyond all expectations. For the study of human behavior and the recording of motion, it has no equal.

We regret that the nature of books precludes the use of motion pictures as illustrative material, and are aware that still photographs of human beings are, from the standpoint of motion, suggestive only. In studying the communicative significance of the ways in which people actually move and act, even direct, first-hand observation leaves a great deal to be desired; the use of motion pictures of real and unstaged events is almost mandatory if accuracy and fresh insights are to be achieved. Few are trained to look steadily and searchingly at the visual world and really to see what passes before the eyes. The nature of action is inherently transitory, and our very familiarity with our everyday surroundings prohibits us from forming an accurate estimate of them. The highly consequential act of putting a "frame" around a person or group or an object concentrates and emphasizes, and there are not many films that deal honestly and directly with real events—films that permit us to look at human beings as they actually are, rather than as a director or cameraman thinks they are or wants to them to appear. Most of the so-called **"documentary" films**, which now include literally thousands of titles, are rich in some falsification, although many of them try to convey in some way or other that they are a "realistic" opposite of the fictional film and although extensive claims are made for their "concern for the world of fact." The films of such documentary producers as the highly praised documentary pioneer Robert Flaherty and his followers Willard Van Dyke, John Grierson, Stuart Legg, Harry Watt, and Arne Sucksdorff have limitations. Their method, with minor exceptions and deviations, has been to choose a subject or theme—the lives of the Eskimos, a Scots shepherd's life during the lambing season, working conditions in British industry, the need for city planning—and to get representative Eskimos, shepherds, workers, and slum dwellers to "reënact" their own roles, often accompanied by a considerable amount of direction from back of the camera. The effect is one of either a flattened-out or a heightened reality, either of which represents a distortion that audiences usually have no way of evaluating.

There are, however, films of a different order altogether that are of the greatest value because of their emphasis on how people actually move and behave, their concern with the ways in which culture, climate, and particular situations determine human movements—films that make it possible, for example, to compare the actions of Germans and Spaniards, schizophrenic children and normal children, and Southern sharecroppers and New York office workers. These are films that actually document, and not "documentaries." Some of the best have been photographed with concealed cameras or with special lenses from such long distances that the subjects have no awareness of being exposed to the scrutiny of the camera. Others have been shot in such places as city streets, playgrounds, and crowds by cameramen with a talent for self-effacement. There is, additionally, a considerable amount of newsreel coverage of events honestly and conscientiously photographed—of war, strikes, riots, disasters, and sports events—that stands in sharp contrast to the obviously reënacted or faked newsreel stories.

Still photography and movie **photography thus distort** in two distinctly different ways. In stills, the onlooker is tempted to believe that the events retained on plate and print existed for some time and perhaps still continue to exist. In movies, the succession of events is predigested, and the onlooker has only to accept or reject the scenes presented to his eye. Characteristic of both is the frame that, from the wealth of material, selects and emphasizes. The still photograph telescopes and distorts time; the movie disguises the emphasis of its producer. Even with these limitations, the photographic technique is ideal for conveying to the observer topics, facts, and details of the "how" that words are incapable of expressing.

Methodology

Until recently scientific knowledge about human communication has been scant. In the past the problem of interrelatedness was taken for granted, dealt with marginally, treated in terms of large generalizations, or was approached as if it were something too mysterious to grasp. Today, however, modern theories and methods have opened the way for coping with many aspects of communication.

Among the various possible methods for an understanding of human communication we have chosen a **clinical** one, with an emphasis upon observation rather than upon scientific experiment and measurement in a laboratory sense. Thus we have avoided the traditional approach to behavior that emphasizes the dissection of the human being into part functions and the separation of mind from body, one person from another, and the individual from the environment. Although such compartmentalization resulted in a vast body of information, it prevented the study of such a pervasive function as human communication, which is difficult to understand as long as rigid barriers between disciplines are maintained. In keeping with the ostensible aim of human communication to establish understanding—that is, correspondence of information between persons—rather than to assure legalistic acuracy of expression, we adapted the methods of assessment to the fluidity of interpersonal processes. Precise methods of measurement are often clumsy and impractical when dealing with human interaction, which is essentially transitory: by the time any statement or action has been accurately recorded and dissected, it has changed, vanished, or moved on, and the analyst is left with nothing but a record of an isolated moment. In the study of human communication, therefore, on-the-spot observations and a method of "evaluation as you go" are, in their approximation, perhaps more relevant than scientific hindsight. To achieve such ends, the student of communication must rigorously train his eyes and ears—and, to a lesser degree, the other sense organs—to deal with whatever stimuli seem relevant. Clinicians who hope to predict future events and to understand or reconstruct those of the past have raised questions as to precisely what should be observed in social interaction. We have attempted to answer some of these questions, using movie and still cameras to suggest the many possible ways of observing movements and gestures, as well as objects.

Within the framework of modern communication theory, communicative actions are conceived of as events that occur in a certain **context.** The perception and evaluation of signals, both spatial and temporal, cannot be separated from the perception and evaluation of the situation in which they occur. A present-day study of communication, therefore, does not aim at compiling a dictionary of gestures or other motions, but instead emphasizes all possible information about the physical and social settings in which the exchange of messages takes place. In addition to considering symbolic movements and gestures and practical, adaptive actions with communicative value, such a study must take into account all those objects with which human beings surround themselves and which affect social interaction.

To document nonverbal communication, we have chosen and limited ourselves to **visually perceivable codifications.** The majority of the illustrations used in this book are from photographs made in the San Francisco Bay area in 1953 and 1954. In our photographic expeditions we wandered from one section to another in an attempt to record human activities and the traces of existence in a variety of situations. Candid and often very rapid shooting was used to capture some of the intentional and unintentional statements made by people as we found them, and by the shopkeepers, decorators, architects, and private home owners whose establishments and houses we saw. We used natural lighting whenever possible. Reflections on store windows or other such blemishes typical of either natural conditions or traces of living were photographed much as any pedestrian might see them.

The pictures were taken with a number of **cameras:** Rolleiflex, Rolleicord, Ansco Reflex, Leica, and Contax. A few of the enlargements come from 16mm negatives taken with a Bell & Howell Filmo 70H camera. A few of the illustrations derived from movies the authors themselves have made (130, 131, 132, 133, 134). We attempted to shoot naturalistically and to edit footage largely in the interest of accurate continuity rather than to inject personal additional touches. That prints from single frames cannot do justice to motion is regrettable but unavoidable.

From an accumulation of several thousand photographs, we selected a few that seemed to convey particularly well the "what" of an observation. Some of these **pictures** were later grouped, so that the total configuration of each group became in itself a nonverbal comment. The choice of each picture dictated in some way the choice of another picture, until we felt we had achieved a sort of self-explanatory "whole," however personal and intuitive our selection. The relatedness of the pictures—either contrasting, complementing, or contradicting—the number used in each group, considerations relating to a saturation point in layout, aesthetic preferences, all were natural outgrowths of this undertaking. It should be pointed out that words rarely do justice to the reactions following the perception of a message codified in pictorial language. Thus the achievement of complete agreement about the "meaning" of a statement coded in this way is not often possible. Readers may consequently disagree with the legends accompanying the pictures, since these are in part descriptive, in part interpretive, and sometimes frankly individual. To reach agreement on matters of interpretation was not our aim. Instead, we have attempted to raise questions and to illustrate a point of view as yet insufficiently exploited.

It should be added that the photographic assessment of visual cues is not aimed at elucidating the psychophysiological problems of perception. We have tried to illustrate how such factors as redundancy in language, the familiarity or strangeness of stimuli, the relationship of things to words, the placement of an object within a framework, the relationship of the state of an organism to a perceived cue, and many other complexly determined total conditions affect communication. In daily life both object and action codifications are not commonly or clearly regarded as a means of communication, and it is precisely for this reason that they are of a particular effectiveness. Occasionally their use makes possible a disguise of intention; at other times, those who use actions and material objects as a medium of communication are, paradoxically, often unaware that they are revealing themselves. Be that as it may, to logicians, linguists, and philosophers our approach may seem insufficiently academic. Even such an objection does not contradict the principal argument we wish to advance: that, **in practice, nonverbal communication must necessarily be dealt with analogically, and this without delay.** Although verbal communication permits a long interval between statements, certain action sequences and gestures necessitate an immediate reply. Then the reaction must be quick and reflexlike, with no time to ponder or to talk. And whenever such a situation occurs, the slower and exhaustive verbal codifications are out of the question for both the actual reply and the scientific method of study.

2. BIOLOGY AND CULTURE AS TWO DETERMINANTS OF NONVERBAL COMMUNICATION

The human functions of communication evolve gradually and are dependent upon the **biological development** of the human being. Genes control the biological growth and decline of organisms. They are the information centers that regulate the gradient of maturation, delineate its limits, and specify the organization of individuals and species (168). The most that environment can contribute to growth is a series of optimal conditions in which the potentialities of the organism can be realized. The communicative abilities of the individual must be properly exercised if they are to reach maximum effectiveness, and the social surroundings of a human being are counted upon to provide an appropriate matrix for the gradual unfolding of the communicative skills of the individual. The people who raise children necessarily abide by certain value systems. **Cultural determinants** are therefore responsible for the choice of language, the nature of the techniques used to manage people, and a host of other factors bearing upon attitudes toward laws, persons, and things and shaping beliefs about birth, death, and religion. But even in a homogeneous sociocultural environment the life experiences of people differ; not all persons have an equal chance to attain full mastery of communicative skills, nor do they all develop in the same direction. In studying people, the scientist is thus faced with a multitude of patterns that he has difficulty in understanding. The difficulties increase greatly when the sociocultural environment is heterogeneous. To find some consistent points of orientation, the scientist therefore searches for invariants—measures, indexes, or principles that could be applied, if not to all, at least to a large number of cases. But it is only natural that he will sometimes attempt to arrive at generalizations bearing upon biological factors on the one hand and sociocultural factors on the other. Although many of the abstractions made about maturation or culture do not fit any individual case completely, the fact still remains that the scientist who has such general information can predict individual behavior with greater accuracy than the person without such knowledge. Therefore generalizations of this kind must be treated as if they were statements of probability rather than statements of individually observed facts. The chances that an eight-year-old is capable of riding a bicycle are definitely greater than if he were a three-year-old; the chances of a German's conceiving of a glorious death in fighting against overwhelming odds are definitely greater than in the case of an American or an Italian.

In the present chapter, two sets of generalizations have been described: first, the development of nonverbal communication in the individual; and second, certain cultural values that favor one kind of nonverbal, gestural expression over another.

The Growth and Decline of Communication in the Life Cycle of Man

Our knowledge of the most favorable conditions contributing to the development of communicative skills in infants is limited, essentially because such a study involves asking questions and getting answers. The theoretical subdivision of problems of communication into such categories as perception, evaluation, and transmission presents major difficulties when the data concern animals or infants, since perception and evaluation are accessible primarily through verbalized accounts of the test subjects or through reports of scientists who themselves assume the roles of guinea pigs. Obviously these methods are out of the question for purposes of studying communication during the first few years of life, and the scientist must confine himself solely to the observation of action—to the movements of both the striped and the smooth muscles, the effects elicited through action in the child himself, and the nonverbal interaction patterns that result.

Motor Development.—The expression of emotions, the ability to make statements, and the transmission of any kind of signals are implemented by the muscles. The communicative process is therefore directly dependent upon the developmental condition of the neuromuscular system. According to Gesell and Amatruda (51), the organization of the effector system begins well before birth, and at the end of the third intrauterine month the fetus is already a moving organism—for example, when a foot meets an obstacle, it withdraws by flection. In the later months of intrauterine development the mother observes slow turning movements involving the trunk, and kicks and jerks involving the extremities. This period, from the twentieth week to the time of delivery, is characterized by successive integration of complex processes rather than by further rapid development of motor functions. However, after birth the motor system develops phenomenally. The lips, tongue, eyes, neck, shoulders, arms, hands, fingers, trunk, legs, feet, and their respective motor functions mature in succession (50). Although hand-mouth and hand-eye coördination achieve a certain level of complexity around the age of five years, it is only between the ages of eight and ten that movements become smooth and poised, hand-eye coördination speedy, and the balance of body and rhythm is finally mastered. The cranial-caudal progression of motor development, the initial learning of gross movement and the later mastery of fine movements, and the final integration of movements involving the sensory system, hands, trunk, and legs determine the ability of the child to express himself at various age levels.

The **development of nonverbal, interpersonal communication** is intimately related to these changes and developments. In the first year of life, expression necessarily must occur through nonverbal means; but even the movements of which the infant is capable are very limited. General reactions involving stimulation of the total autonomic nervous system predominate over the stimulation of the central nervous system. The child literally "speaks" with his whole body, though it is by no means impossible that the symbolization process in the child's mind is ahead of his ability to express information by means of either actions or words. At each developmental level, statements are expressed through the media that are momentarily of importance because they are being learned, practiced, and rehearsed. Modes of expression through action differ at various age levels. Children move muscle groups according to their need to practice motions they are in the process of learning. At first, when sucking, biting, and clutching are the only available expressions, communication by necessity is interpersonal and carried on at close range. By movements of the hand, through rocking motions of the whole body, and by manipulation of the nipple, a mother conveys messages to her baby; through sucking, biting, crying, and smiling, the baby responds. Later, when locomotion develops, the child's statements are expressed through creeping, walking, and running; when the vocabulary is expanding, words seem to be unduly emphasized.

In early infancy the child is dependent upon the muscular assistance of the adult. The incomplete and undifferentiated movements of the child are interpreted and then completed by his parents; a crying baby, as if he had pushed a button, sets a whole machinery of adult help into motion. Conversely, the adult creates situations in which the infant can practice his limited movements. In the early stages of communication the mother interprets silence, sleep, and expressions of satisfaction as affirmative responses, and crying as a negative response. Although speech gradually takes on more and more importance, communication mediated through action continues to be of significant importance until the child does not need the physical assistance of the adult any longer, because it is primarily for purposes of getting help that the child uses nonverbal communication. This stage is certainly not reached before the age of ten, and perhaps is closer to twelve or fourteen. By this time physical assistance given by the adult is gradually transformed into an assistance that involves the transfer of information. Thus around the time of adolescence the gradual switch in the means of codification seems to have been completed: old action codifications are largely relinquished, and instead the verbal, gestural, and symbolic means of communication predominate.

Difficulties arise when parents are not flexible in communicating nonverbally and fail to respond at each age level with appropriate motions. An impoverishment of communication and character development can be observed in those children who grew up in surroundings where the verbal was emphasized too early and where messages expressed in nonverbal terms were left unanswered.

Speech Development.—Speech is one of the last of the functions to develop and mature. At the age of eighteen most anatomical structures of the body have reached a point of development beyond which they will not progress noticeably, but the larynx continues to develop during maturity. The hardening of the cartilaginous tissues, which is responsible for changes in the voice, continues well into adult years. The reasons for this slow process are obvious: before speech and language functions develop, a number of other functions must reach a satisfactory maturation stage (96). The first of these functions is the infant's ability to discriminate among sounds of high pitch that invest speech tones with their particular characteristics. Second is his acquisition of a memory span to encompass individual speech sounds. Third is the acquisition of motor speech, for speech is based upon movements so rapid that the child's motor maturation has to be well advanced before he can successfully attempt to imitate adult language. To utter meaningful sounds, the child must be able not only to execute specialized movements but to coördinate these specialized movements rapidly. Finally, the use of speech as a method of implementing future action is also related to the acquisition of frustration tolerance. As long as this tolerance is low, communication between the child and the adult is mediated primarily through perception and expression of simple movements and simple sounds. As the tolerance of frustration on the part of the child increases, speech and more time-consuming elaborations become more prominent.

The first infant **sounds** employ only large muscle groups and do not require any particular shaping of the tongue. Later, specialized movements require use of the mandible, lips, and tip of the tongue; subsequently, there are those that depend upon the soft palate and the back of the tongue (92). The child first learns to produce sounds whose changes in pitch and intensity vary with the words or phrases, and only later does he learn to add meaningful plosive, sibilant, and fricative noises produced by the apparatus of articulation. The first words to be developed are primitive interjections, followed by nouns, action verbs, and adjectives. Most children—even those who develop late—have begun to speak at least by the time they are three and a half years old, unless they suffer from an abnormality. All speech sounds are developed by the time the child is seven; however, on the whole, language habits develop more rapidly in girls than in boys, and fewer girls have speech defects (161). The eight-year-old uses language fluently and excessively, is interested in reading, listens to verbal accounts on the radio, begins to use codes and secret languages, verbalizes ideas, and is capable of verbally localizing bodily complaints. Finally, at eight or nine, he begins to use language for purposes of strategy, and the faculty of critical thinking emerges gradually (49, 120).

The motor development of speech and the coördination of sensory and motor components are thus more or less completed within the first decade of life, at the same time that the coördination of other bodily movements, balance, and the mastery of the fine muscle movements are achieved. However, an additional decade is required to learn the strategic cues of human interaction, and perhaps even more time to become skilled in the making of decisions (103).

Communication and Interaction.—From the time of conception, it may be assumed, communication exists between the ovum and its surroundings. The processes of maturation in the fetus, although largely controlled by the genes, are nonetheless in some ways influenced by stimuli originating in the maternal organism. The spectrum of stimuli, primarily composed of mechanical, thermal, and chemical signals, changes at birth as the infant is directly exposed to sound, light, and air. This change in spectrum to auditory, visual, and tactile stimuli necessitates, however, an additional important step. **In utero** the child is in a state of permanent contiguity with the mother, and therefore is directly or indirectly affected by the experiences of the mother. When mother and child physically separate, the child may be exposed to stimuli that do not reach the mother, and vice versa. Not only new, but intense stimuli reach the child's sense organs. In the **first three months** of postnatal life, negative expressional movements predominate. For example, the head may be thrown back and turned away, the hands of the mother may be pushed away, the nipple may be forced out of the mouth; screaming or crying may prevent feeding. During this period, auditory stimuli in particular produce negative reactions. Sounds of slight intensity are not reacted to, and almost every external stimulus of more than minimal intensity likewise produces negative reactions (21, 72). Positive expressional movements such as glowing eyes, arms outstretched toward an object, and smiling, and such vocalizations as crowing, shouting, babbling, and laughter, show marked increase in the third month.

In the first few months of life the infant changes from a sensory reactor to a social organism. At four weeks, the infant quiets down when picked up; at eight weeks, smiles at the sight of a face; and at sixteen weeks, recognizes his mother. By the time the child is five months old, he dislikes being left alone and cries when people leave. In subsequent months the relationship to the mother is still further elaborated, and at the end of the first year personalized interaction with her has been firmly established. This development culminates in the five-year-old, who is well adjusted, on intimate terms with his mother, and capable of dealing successfully with one person at a time.

Infancy

1

FROM BABYHOOD TO OLD AGE

Childhood

Adolescence

Adulthood

The later years

The six-year-old, faced with **school**, meets an entirely new situation (52). The previous smooth relation with his mother becomes somewhat strained, and he begins to take more cognizance of his father and children of his own age. Almost all the next ten years are spent in establishing himself in the group. Obviously **group communication** differs from interpersonal communication (128). In a conversation between two persons one message follows another, reception alternates with transmission, and correction and feedback are more or less immediate. Communication in a group, in contrast, is more rigidly organized, and complex rules and multiple roles present more involved problems. Different individuals must be dealt with simultaneously, and the role of self becomes subordinated to the task of group. Correction of information may be delayed, or replies completely missing. Tentatively at first the child's attention is devoted to group activities only for the briefest periods. Children under five have been observed associating in groups of two or three other children for anywhere from ten to forty minutes. When children are between five and seven, the time span goes as high as from one to three hours. The peak of group development is not reached until adolescence, when from one-half to two-thirds of all youths between eleven and seventeen belong to groups (24).

In **adolescence**, interpersonal and group communication coexist. Interpersonal communication, as it prevailed in the first few years of life, is resumed with new vigor. But instead of involving one or both parents, the adolescent now relates to either a member of the opposite sex or perhaps a slightly older member of the same sex. Finally, when the child becomes a **young adult**, he assumes the privileges and responsibilities of society. Now a new system of communication must be learned, which involves dealing with persons of all ages and differing status, origins, backgrounds, and occupations. Because of this heterogeneity, it may take five or ten years before the age of communicative maturity is reached—usually around the age of thirty. Frequently it occurs only after the young adult has become a parent himself and is forced to understand the communication system of his children.

In the **fourth and fifth decades**, particularly in the middle class, another change in the patterns of communication occurs. Persons in positions of responsibility, parents, and middle-aged persons in general do not strive so much for the acquisition of information and refinement of communicative skills as they implement their information in positions of control and decision making. The cycle thus shifts from roles concerned with input and output to those involving evaluation of policies and decisions that concern other people and group interests.

The initial development of symbolization systems depends upon stimulation that may be excessive and actions that may be exhausting. Limiting biological changes demand, however, that **older persons** protect themselves from new and extreme stimulation and consequent fatigue and exhaustion. The learning of new symbolization systems at this age is therefore extremely limited. Unless the middle-aged person is mature in terms of communication, he is likely to undergo a process of impoverishment, with a concomitant loss of joy in living, through the scarcity of new information and the absence of stimulating human relations. Conversely, those who are equipped with communicative skills can enjoy life well into the eighth and ninth decades. In old age, finally, positions of responsibility are gradually relinquished, and time is increasingly spent in reminiscence of the past.

THE DEVELOPMENT OF COMMUNICATION

(Chronological time scales subject to wide individual variation and are used for purposes of illustration only.)

Intrauterine period: (40 weeks)	Organism responds to thermal, mechanical, and chemical stimuli.
Neonatal period: (first 12 weeks)	Infant learns to respond to tactile, auditory, and visual stimuli.
Babyhood: (3 to 24 months)	Mastery of head, eye, and hand movements (second quarter); trunk and fingers (third quarter); legs and feet (fourth quarter); speech (second year).
Infancy: (2 to 5 years)	Interpersonal communication with one person at a time (mother, father, sibling, or relative).
Later childhood: (6 to 12 years)	Group communication with several persons at a time, especially with children of the same age and with emphasis on members of the same sex.
Adolescence: (12 to 18 years)	Interpersonal communication with members of opposite sex; growing attempts to communicate with members of out-groups.
Young adulthood: (19 years to late twenties)	Mastery of the complexity and heterogeneity of adult communication and the multiplicity of roles and diversity of rules. Communication with age superiors; the young adult is occupationally placed in a position of subservience; observes and follows orders.
Middle adulthood: (late twenties to middle forties)	Peak of communication with age inferiors and children. Switch from role of perceiver and transmitter to position of greater responsibility.
Later adulthood: (45 to 65 years)	Intake of information and learning now displaced in favor of output of information, teaching, governing, and ruling. Participation in decision-making groups.
Age of retirement: (65 to 80 years)	Preparation for relinquishment of power and gradual retirement from decision making. Philosophical considerations toward the end of life cycle. Symbolic and global treatment of events.
Old age: (80+ years)	Life in retrospect, with emphasis on early memories.

Nonverbal Communication in Cultural Perspective

Most persons interested in movements can identify individuals belonging to certain national, cultural, occupational, or social class groups. The sailor's rolling gait, the Prussian officer's clipped movements, the catlike motions of certain Pacific islanders are well-known stereotypes. It is not surprising, therefore, that numerous attempts have been made to relate gestures and movements to **racial types.** The aim has always been to single out movements that investigators thought to be characteristic of their hypothetical norms. The complete failure of these attempts to establish genetically determined and racially linked movement types was to be expected. Most claims to the existence of such types were purely speculative, based on insufficient evidence, without a description of techniques of observation or adequate controls (36).

The attempt to link gesture and movement to particular cultures was not much more successful (75, 148). In the tradition of nineteenth-century thought, characteristic movements were assigned to such hypothetical **cultural caricatures** as the "typical Neapolitan" or the "typical Englishman," or attempts were made to isolate a "typical Neapolitan" or a "typical English" set of gestures. But these generalizations fail to stand up when such sub-groupings as social classes or occupational settings are taken into account. Efron (36), for example, found that, in comparative studies of Eastern Jews and southern Italians in New York City, the more assimilated the individuals were, the less characteristic their Jewish or Italian gestural traits became. In other words, such gestures lost their identifying qualities and blended with those present in the milieu in which the individuals lived. Observations on "hybrid" gesticulation indicate that the same individuals, if exposed for a period of time to two or more gesturally different groups, may adopt and combine certain gestural traits of both groups. These findings clearly indicate that gesture and movement are a function of the communication system of which an individual is a part, and that a gesture can be understood only when the communication system as a whole is assessed.

Comparative anthropological studies have shown that actions and gestures, with perhaps the sole exception of expressions of extreme emotion, are on the whole dependent upon explicit or implicit prior agreements. The Japanese smile is not necessarily a spontaneous expression of amusement, but a law of etiquette. The Japanese also consider it necessary to censor love scenes in American movies because they regard kissing as an act of private love play that arouses disgust when indulged in publicly. Conversely, hissing in Japan is a sign of polite deference to social superiors, whereas in England as well as in America it is the exact opposite—a sign of extreme disapproval (86).

On a societal plane, the communication system of a nation or any of its subdivisions ostensibly serves to insure the well-being and survival of its citizens, and the organization of the communication network and the modes of communication are fitted to suit typical and recurring situations. The typical element is usually not so much a single gesture or a single action, but the patterning of various symbolic and adaptive expressions. The pattern can often be identified on an abstract level only, either in terms of timing, rhythm, repetition, or in terms of spatial arrangements or context. For example, variations in climate, the density of population, the prevalence of either an agricultural or an industrial economy, the availability of raw materials, the historical past, and many other factors, will all determine in part the varieties of communication. In any culture each person is prepared, therefore, through education to assume a place in the communication network of his particular group, and the cumulative body of experience of generations reflects itself in the expressions of the individual. This particular thesis—the subservience of movement and gesture to long-range values —is illustrated below with examples drawn from five different cultures. Gesture among the Americans is largely oriented toward activity; among the Italians it serves the purposes of illustration and display; among the Jews it is a device of emphasis; among the Germans it specifies both attitude and commitment; and among the French it is an expression of style and containment.

To be more detailed, the basic value system of most present-day Anglo-Saxon **Americans** (127), most strikingly among the middle class, emphasizes such activities as keeping occupied, being enterprising, striving for achievement, and being entertained. On the basis of such a valuation of action, people engage in trade and in the production of goods, are concerned to various extents with social progress, and seek "relaxation" through spectator sports, games, locomotion, the moving pictures, popular magazines and books, and—to a much lesser extent—physical exercise. Madariaga (99) says that the British are generally men of action rather than men of thought; this observation applies to the Americans as well. The whole tendency can perhaps be best illustrated by such men as Daniel Boone, Henry Ford, and Benjamin Franklin, all of whose careers symbolize a strain of American life that contrasts sharply with a far less representative one exemplified by such men as Whistler, Veblen, and Henry James. In such a culture of action, symbolic and verbal expression is not usually regarded as an end in itself but tends to be implemental and practical. Political speeches, newspaper editorials, and the remarks of radio commentators consequently may not reflect what their writers actually believe. Hence, implicit nonverbal communication as it is used by the American "man in the street" is of the essence, and unstated assumptions assume a greater importance.

In the study of gestural movements and actions of Americans, it should be kept in mind that the framework is one in which the emphasis is generally upon doing rather than upon esthetic or speculative questioning of what is done. But the subject is an elusive one: in a country made up of so many national and racial strains, and subject to such a variety of regional influences, generalizations are hazardous. The differences are likely to be profound between the gestures and actions of a Louisiana Negro who works in the sugar fields and those of a New York white-collar worker of Anglo-Saxon descent; even the timing of such gestures as may be commonly shared is likely to be strikingly different. It is probably safe to say, however, that gestures seeming to be uniquely indigenous to America are, in general, lacking in the ardent stylization of those of the French or the interpersonal involvements conveyed through Italian gestures. Such typically American gestures as the hitchhiking sign— which could, incidentally, originate only in a country where total strangers are welcomed as passengers—or the bull's-eye sign designate more often than not the direction or intensity of movement or the effect and success of action; but few such gestures or actions contain a subjective reference indicating frustration or gratification.

In contrast to Americans, present-day **Italians** live in a climate of passionate emotional expression. The basic philosophy of this Mediterranean country is epitomized by a desire to express bodily and emotional needs in elaborate and somewhat outspoken terms while at the same time maintaining warm interpersonal contact. Throughout the centuries, the physical expression of the Italians has been stabilized in a tradition of intense interpersonal relations. From the Roman Empire through the Renaissance to the present, the country's architecture, sculpture, and painting, and—to a lesser degree—music, reflect such a heritage. The essential emphasis has been upon the nonverbal; Italy's contributions to literature, with the exception of Dante, are secondary to its achievements in nonverbal artistic forms, which are epitomized in the works of such diversely gifted men as Michelangelo and Leonardo.

Italian movements are essentially carried out by the face, the arms, and the shoulders, and rarely by the hips and lower extremities. Italians are notorious for their dislike of walking. Among their greatest achievements have been those in which hands and facial expression have been combined with oratory. Gestures are used to illustrate and characterize movement in the midst of talking, to the extent of substituting gestures for words. The gestures of the hands are executed in a lateral transversal plane; according to Efron (36), grasping, poking, pulling, and shaking of other persons are rarely observed among Italians. When

Italians meet in groups, they do not stand close together, but rather apart, since the radius of their arm movements is sweeping. These incline to be smooth, and transitions in tempo occur gradually. In Italy simultaneous gesturing seems to be rare; gestures are seldom employed for purposes of interruption, but rather for mutual reassurance. The Italian uses gestures that tend to be pictorial or physiographic; they tend to imitate or reënact the actions that are verbally described. Generally, Italian gesture tends to be emphatic, illustrative, redundant, and flamboyant, and probably has changed little in character since the time of the early Romans (148). Expression for purposes of making oneself clear or for purposes of deceit is actually a sport practiced by everyone. Any kind of action is likely to be used primarily for communicative purposes and only secondarily in order to get things done.

Jewish gestures have been subjected to a similar close scrutiny (36). Since Jewish tradition is one of the oldest in existence, it lends itself particularly well to a comparison of movements and value systems. Jewish culture has been characterized through the ages by a search for laws to regulate human intercourse. Despite profound differences in the basic ideologies of Moses, Christ, the Apostles, Marx, and Freud, all have in common the yearning to organize relations within the in-group.

In both the Old and the New Testaments the in-group is a chosen people; with Marx, a rigidly delineated industrial proletariat; with Freud, the closed circle of orthodox Freudians. It is worth noting that no attempts were made in terms of this over-all philosophy to tolerate differences or to include the out-group. The only hope held out to members of the out-group was to accept the values of the in-group.

The exceedingly verbal Jewish culture prefers digital to analogic codifications. In their ways of communication the Jews pay little attention to the nonverbal symbolic, and use movement largely to support words. Gesture is used almost exclusively for purposes of interpunctuation or emphasis, and can be rhetorically characterized as a gesture of address. Gesticulation is aimed directly at another person and usually carried out with the lower arm, the upper arm being rigidly held to the side of the body. Legs and hips are rarely involved. Tempo is frequently jerky, and such contactual gestures as grasping, poking, pulling, and shaking are frequently employed. The members of a colloquial group generally stand close together, frequently gesticulating together. According to Efron (36), the Jewish gestures are predominantly of the discursive or ideographic type—a kind of gestural portrayal, not of the object of reference or thought, but of the process of logic itself. The accompanying movement results in a complex embroidering, underlining, punctuating, accenting, italicizing, and catapulting.

Whereas the Anglo-Saxon and Italian cultures are highly nonverbal and the Jewish and French exceedingly verbal, the **German** culture holds an intermediate position. The greatest contributions of the Germans have been in the fields of philosophy, science, and music. But unlike the French, who were concerned with problems of living and taste, the Germans tended to specialize in transcendental philosophies exemplified by such names as Kant, Fichte, and Hegel. German attitudes toward belief were associated with an authoritarian family structure, relegation of the woman to a secondary position, and a strong emphasis on hero worship. It is not surprising, consequently, that gesture and posture were used primarily for the expression of intrapsychic events and secondarily for purposes of interpersonal communication. The German language itself attests to this fact by having more words for subtle, intrapsychic events than any other language in Western civilization. Since interpersonal sensitivity does not guide the exchange of messages, the Germans need to establish rigid rules of conduct that regulate group and interpersonal relationships. Communication in German culture is thus shaped by ideas of rigid order and law. Devotion to duty often takes the place of understanding one another, and German gestures are, therefore, not so much signals for communicating details as they are metacommunicative statements about personal assumptions, roles, and social position. Many Germans, especially the Prussians, try to emulate their military heroes, and much of the soldierlike posture and movement has been adopted by the population at large. Compared with the French, most Germans appear clumsy. The most expressive areas of their bodies are the face and the region of the spine; the eyes and mouth are used to show "the innermost depths of the soul." The other movements of the body are markedly angular and incisive, and whatever gestures are carried out by the hand or the arm are to reinforce statements about belief. Gesture and posture are thus aimed more at idiosyncratic expression and largely used to make statements "to whom it may concern" than employed for purposes of specific and well-directed communication.

The basic communicative philosophy of the **French** reveals itself in the desire to display style and taste in word, gesture, and action. For many centuries France's role as a pace setter for Western civilization was based upon the intense emphasis it gave to the refinement of systems of symbolization and their application to human relations (79, 99). French style and taste, originating in court ideas of chivalry, intrigue, polished words, and accomplished formality, were readily taken over by the ruling classes of the entire Continent. Aspects that assumed importance were such things as food and dress and the elegance of human conduct. But with the advent of the French Revolution and the change in social structure, some of the emphasis on style, taste, and conduct became outmoded and empty gestures, recalling past days but not adapted to modern conditions.

Foremost among the core values of French culture is the emphasis on thought, and in no other country have speech and writing been taken so seriously. Verbal expression reached its climax in the novel, satire, drama, poetry, memoirs, aphorisms, and correspondence; the intricacies of thought were expounded in countless treatises on philosophy and mathematics, or even in the Code Napoléon. In keeping with the precision of their writing, the French use movements sparingly; gestures are neither as expansive as those of the Italians nor as insistent as those of the Jews, nor are they used with the casualness of the Americans, nor do they show such rigor as those of the Germans. Gestures are stylized expressions of emotions, calculated and executed with elegance and precision. More than in other cultures, emotional expression is related to the total behavior of a person, although minute details of face and fingers are brilliantly brought into play. It is more the sequence of whole actions which are interpreted as gestures. Comportment in a social situation is the embodiment of the French gesture; it is neither interpersonal nor illustrative, but essentially serves the purpose of carrying expression to an ideal perfection.

3. THE VARIETIES OF NONVERBAL LANGUAGES

Probably some tens of thousands of years elapsed between the beginning of speech and the first appearance of writing. But no record of this evolution appears until the emergence of Sumerian, a language spoken in the Mesopotamian valley between 4000 B.C. and 300 B.C. Almost as old are the records of the Akkadian language of the Babylonians and Assyrians who invaded the Sumerian territory about 3000 B.C. Of somewhat more recent origin are those of ancient China and Egypt, dating back to about 2000 B.C. The oldest written records among Indo-European languages are the Vedic hymns in Sanskrit (2000 B.C.), *The Iliad* and *The Odyssey* in Greek (800 B.C.), and a variety of inscriptions in Latin (500 B.C.) (118).

Compared to these relatively recent records, our knowledge of **ancient man** from other evidence dates back much further than 4000 B.C. The oldest findings of what are believed to be parts of human skeletons have been ascribed to the beginning of the Pleistocene, almost a million years ago; the skeleton of the Galley Hill man, essentially a type of modern man, is believed to be at least half a million years old (104). The conclusion that these skeletons are human is based, not only upon morphological characteristics of bones and calculation of brain volume, but upon the fact that anthropologists found these skeletons together with implements of various kinds.

The earliest remains of man's material culture are almost entirely crude **articles of stone**. Sometimes it is impossible to tell whether forms regarded as implements are the work of man or of nature. Although there are authorities who doubt that some of the anthropological findings can be attributed to the upper Miocene, certainty of human remains increases in the Pliocene, and doubts cease in the Pleistocene. It is precisely at this latter period that Galley Hill man lived. Implements of this period are indeed crude, but their forms are such as to preclude the possibility that they are accidental freaks of nature. At later periods and with progressive evolution, implements became more complex: when hafting was invented, wood could be joined with stone; when paste was discovered, molding led to the development of pottery; the discovery of leverage led to foundations for building; twining, lashing, knotting, and weaving formed the basis for clothing (157). But whether these objects were crude or refined, primitive or complex, they—in combination with whole skeletons, skulls, and jaws—constitute the only remains of ancient man. The history of the evolution of implements (56, 157) is therefore at the same time a record of the development of human types of codification and symbolization. Prehistoric man communicates to us down through the ages by means of object language; whereas the physical anthropologist searches for examples of such early statements made by man, paleontologists and geologists use object language in very much the same way to explore periods antedating the history of man for hundreds of millions of years. Fossils assume the role of skeletons and implements in this connection.

The paleontology of culture, **archaeology,** concerns itself with the beginnings of organized society (67). The traces left by the Egyptians, Greeks, and Romans are infinitely more numerous than those left by earlier men; but the increase of our information about these Mediterranean cultures is not only due to the presence of written records but is also due to the complexity of the material culture. The multiplicity of objects, the remains of larger material aggregates such as ancient houses, or the ruins of whole cities (167) enable us to see how object was related to object and part to whole. From the single stone objects found in the eolithic and paleolithic periods, continuing through the multiple stone objects found in the neolithic period, we have, in historical times, successively passed through the bronze, iron, steel, and electronic stages of object collections. Primitive and single objects give us information about the manual activities of the men who used them. The organization of space in terms of roads, houses, temples, and market places reveals how particular activities may have been carried out in a social setting.

Even the combination of object with architectural evidence is, however, still incomplete and unsatisfactory, and not until remains of an unmistaken symbolic character are found are we able more fully to reconstruct the value systems of the past. The first complete series of symbolic records dates back some forty thousand years, when cave men (19) covered their walls with the most delicate engravings, drawings, and paintings of animals. But what has come down to us in terms of reproductions of human beings is scant, and not until the time of the first written records do we find pictorial records set forth with some abundance. Thus at the point when man learned to use objects symbolically, when he represented human beings in paintings, murals, or sculpture, and when he began to write, the archaeologist partly relinquishes his task as interpreter of the past. His role is taken over by **historians** of art and political and personal history—specialists in the symbolic expressions of earlier civilizations.

Objects convey information. Just as spoken language transmitted by radio and television bridges the spatial gap between people, object language bridges the gap of time. Objects—some of them at least—are enduring, and the information coded in material items has survived for centuries. Our cumulative knowledge of the evolution of the earth, of man, and of society has all been reconstructed from information coded in object language; and although probably none of the men who left food and weapons in the graves of their dead thought that these articles would convey messages to later generations, they nonetheless considered them necessary, either for identification of the dead or for furnishing means of subsistence on the trip to the beyond. It is purely coincidental that other men would reopen these graves in search of knowledge after thousands of years, and that the intended "beyond" conceived in spatial terms should turn out to be a "later" in temporal terms.

In the reconstruction of the past two things were still missing. No sound of ancient times had been heard; no minutely accurate record of motion had reached posterity. In the nineteenth and the twentieth centuries this gap was finally closed. As movies and sound recordings were developed, the dynamic qualities of human action could be captured and almost every visual impression retained, along with contemporary sounds and voices. News photography, film coverage, telecasts, and tape today record much of what is thought to be significant in the world, and these records in turn will be handed on to future generations.

Pictorial Languages

A **pictograph** (39) is a pictorial symbol denoting a real object, person, group, or institution. Primitive systems of writing employed by the Egyptians, Sumerians, Assyrians, Babylonians, Chinese, and Cretans were originally based on such simple pictorial signs, which resemble those used by American Indians (156) and Australian natives. But since depictable objects did by no means satisfactorily express qualifications, actions, or ideas, the ideograph developed, which denoted a combination of actions and ideas; for example, the combination of the pictographs for "sun" and "moon" was used to signify "light." Eventually several ideographs were combined to form still more complicated ideographs; those representing faith, piety, temperance, and justice were condensed in a symbol conveying the idea of virtue. The great advantage of pictorial representation was that, regardless of pronunciation or dialect, the symbolization remained the same; ancient people of different tongues thus were able to communicate through writing without difficulty, although they may have been incapable of understanding each other through speech (118). Pictographic and ideographic systems of writing ordinarily have little influence upon the spoken language; in nomadic civilizations or in periods of culture change, these systems have been unrivaled for communicating with out-groups.

Phonetic systems of writing are generally more accurate, simpler, and faster; they influence the spoken word, they introduce stability and tradition, but they can be understood only by the in-group. The people living near the Euphrates, the Tigris, and the Nile eventually discovered the advantage of using letters to represent single sounds (138). The Egyptians were probably the first to combine phonetic denotation with hieroglyphics, but it remained for the Phoenicians and Hebrews to perfect the phonetic alphabet. From Phoenicia the system of sound representation of speech was carried to Greece, and then on to the Etruscans and the Romans. Although Latin is the root of all our Western systems of writing, Arabic—equally derived from the Phoenicians and the Hebrews—became the basis for many forms of writing in the Near and Middle East and in India.

Pictographs and ideographs are by no means defunct. Contemporary Chinese script developed from pictorial representation, much as did some forms of our own scientific denotation systems. Among more recent developments in pictorial languages, which have become internationally standardized, are the floral diagrams of botanists, the pictorial symbols for the structure of molecules used in chemical literature, and the graphic symbols employed in electric wiring diagrams. A modern universal picture language applicable to a variety of fields is the Isotype, which is used particularly for the presentation of social statistics.

Another form of pictorial language appears in the development of contemporary **comic strips** (68, 82). Although there is a long tradition of satirical art, popularized in cartoons during the spread of journalism in the nineteenth century, the language of the "funnies"—a combination of words and cartoons to tell a continued story—first appeared in "The Yellow Kid" in the *New York World* in 1896. With the publication of "Mutt and Jeff" (1907), newspapers began to feature comic strips regularly, later introducing color on Sundays (147,

2

A MODERN PICTOGRAPH

THE INVENTION OF
THE AUTOMOBILE

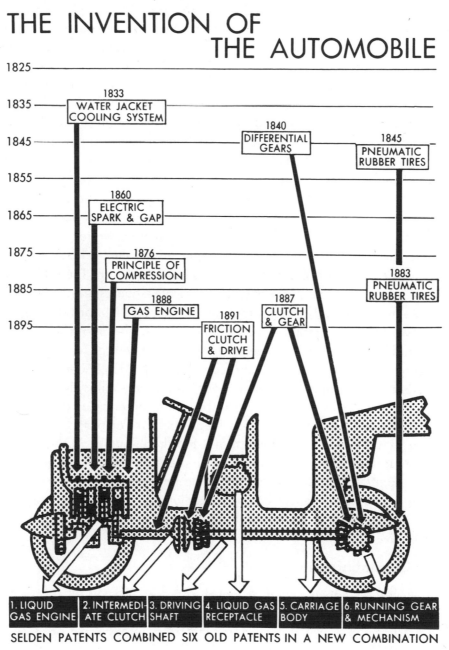

SELDEN PATENTS COMBINED SIX OLD PATENTS IN A NEW COMBINATION

PICTOGRAPH CORPORATION

THE ISOTYPE

159). The creators of the modern strips have introduced devices of their own, indicating what such characters as Moon Mullins and Major Hoople, for example, are thinking with words encircled by a cloudlike form hovering above their heads. Speed in movement is denoted by streaks indicating blur of vision or dust, surprise by exclamation points, and bewilderment by a question mark. Such combinations of the verbal and the pictorial are capable of delineating actions, moods, and sentiments that even extensive verbal treatment could not accomplish. The captionless cartoon is a later development, making its points exclusively through nonverbal methods. As developed by *The New Yorker* and in the work of such men as Otto Soglow, Charles Addams, Saul Steinberg, and James Thurber, a new precision of wit through immediacy was emphasized. This immediacy is probably due to the innate differences in the treatment of time in pictorial denotation as opposed to the phonetic one. Pictorial representation usually deals only with given moments, whereas phonetic denotation emphasizes the element of time in much the same way that musical denotation does. Written music denotes changes in frequency vibrations of tone over time, whereas written language indicates spoken sounds over time. In magazine and newspaper advertising, on posters, and on billboards, an amalgam of the pictorial and the verbal is seldom missing. The subject matter of a statement is ordinarily identified pictorially; the predicate—and especially statements about thinking and feeling—is usually elaborated upon in words. Billboard and television advertisers have discovered that, in terms of dollars and cents, a message is more effective in producing immediate sales when verbal denotation is mixed with pictorial or object language.

The evolution from pictographic through ideographic to phonetic denotation in the course of hundreds and thousands of years is paralleled by a similar **development in the individual** human being. A six-month-old baby will appreciate a rattle or a teddy bear—in brief, the thing itself. The three- or four-year-old looks at picture books, and may realize that the pictures stand for something that is not there; finally, in the first grade at the age of six, the child learns phonetic denotation in the study of reading and writing. Every child draws and paints for several years before he begins to deal with letters. Pictorial representation in this sense is connected with an earlier step of development; phonetic denotation requires greater experience, because it depends upon the analysis and abstraction of part functions of events.

Art and Communication

Painting, sculpture, dancing, and acting all represent nonverbal forms of communication. Sometimes the message is addressed to a single person; more often it is a statement to many. But in order to be interpreted, the assumptions of a historical period as well as the assumptions of the individual artist must be understood. From the standpoint of communication, therefore, creative arts have two important aspects: first, that they represent nonverbal forms of codification; and second, that they are deeply concerned with the metacommunicative—that is, with the assumptions that must be made in order to understand the artist's statement. Art both codifies and interprets. Only by means of drawings, paintings, sculpture, and photography are we able to get an inkling of how people who lived at a given period attempted to symbolize—or inadvertently succeeded in symbolizing—thoughts, feelings, or even the entire pattern of their lives. Symbolic representation in art is therefore more than merely a code; it always contains a comment, an interpretation, and a suggestion of how to understand its symbols. The embodiment of an idea into a work of art contains both communicative and metacommunicative messages. The Christ of a Grünewald, in this sense, conveys primarily ideas of agony; the Christ of an Epstein, Hebraic monumentality; and the Christ of contemporary calendar art, a sense at once cloying and artificial.

The **first works of art** had a highly practical purpose. Early man decorated his weapons with carvings and the walls of his caves with pictures of animals, probably with the intention of being representational (76). Sculptors of Egypt and Greece (108, 122), in contrast, were set the task of creating statues of the gods, which assumed the forms of human beings, in a highly idealized manner. This art was primarily interpretive. As the narrower views of the older Greek civilization gave way to the broader and more cosmopolitan outlook of the Hellenistic world, the naturalistic treatment of the body in Greek sculpture increased, since a closer and more extensive study of anatomy was taking place. Artists grasped a widening comprehension of nature, and shifted from a world of form into one of space filled with depths of shadow and gleaming light, from a world of sculpture into one of painting (124).

The **Middle Ages** offer still another realignment. Under Church domination, art's chief function was that of putting across Christian teachings and beliefs to the illiterate. Divine qualities and theological concepts had to be communicated in terms of concrete images. Brushes were ceaselessly occupied in the production of madonnas and angels. Although symbolic values were emphasized at the expense of the representational and the dramatic, the artists—particularly in mosaic decoration and book illustration—made use of intense primary colors and backgrounds of gold whose ornamental power and emotional values communicate themselves with force and immediacy.

With the advent of the **Renaissance** the appreciation of the image itself began, quite separate from the idea, person, or god it represented (101). The distinction between craftsman and intellectual began to disappear with the emergence of such accomplished and unspecializing personalities as Leonardo da Vinci and Michelangelo. Life became experimental and adventurous, and men looked at the world as though seeing it in an entirely fresh light. Art began to be thought of as a quasi science, and the view that art imitates nature became the guiding concept.

From the high Renaissance to the middle of the nineteenth century, the viewpoint from which artists regarded their world and the terms in which they communicated it are, from a long-range viewpoint, relatively unvaried. The **impressionists,** however, departed from the traditional approach. Their major revolution was to paint directly in the presence of nature instead of working, as the old masters did, from notes and drawings in a studio. In this sense they were more immediately affected by nature than earlier artists. The consequence was a quality of light and color not achieved before. New discoveries about the laws of color were applied by the artists, muddy color was discarded, and color was broken up and made to work for the sake of the entire canvas. Impressionism had a moral aspect as well. Meyer Schapiro says: "It is remarkable how many pictures we have in early Impressionism of informal and spontaneous sociability, of breakfasts, picnics, promenades, boating trips, holidays, and vacation travel. These urban idylls not only present the objective forms of bourgeois recreation in the 1860's and 1870's; they also reflect in the very choice of subjects and in the new esthetic devices the conception of art as solely a field of individual enjoyment . . ." (139).

With Cézanne modern painting moved in the direction of **abstract and nonobjective art.** Many earlier painters had taken for granted that the worth of a picture ultimately rests in colors and shapes alone. "In renouncing or drastically distorting natural shapes the abstract painter makes a judgment of the external world. He says that such and such aspects of experience are alien to art and to the higher realities of form; he disqualifies them from art. But by this very act, the mind's view of itself and of its art, the intimate contexts of this repudiation of objects, become directing factors in art" (139). Painting moves toward the purity and refinement of music and geometry (78); in doing so, even though eliminating the image of man, it still speaks to those men who can read the language of paint (77).

An altogether different approach in art is encountered in those forms in which the human body is used directly for artistic expression. Foremost of these is the **dance;** historically regarded, it is not only the first of all the arts, but the only one in which the creator and the creation are not separated. Curt Sachs says: "Rhythmical patterns of movement, the plastic sense of space, the vivid representation of a world seen and imagined—these things man creates in his own body in the dance before he uses substance and stone and word to give expression to his inner experiences" (135).

Sachs makes an initial distinction between dances that are in harmony with the body and those that are not. Of the latter variety, the convulsive and jerky dances of some tribes "correspond to the description of clonic convulsion—the state of forceful flexion and relaxation of the muscles which may lead to a throwing about of the body in wild paroxysms. The will has completely or to a certain extent lost control over the parts of the body; consciousness may likewise completely disappear." On the other hand, the dance that is in harmony with the body, though by no means lacking in exhilaration and ecstasy, originates "in an irrepressible delight in motor expression," is marked by exaltation rather than mortification of the flesh, and "calls the movements of all parts of the body into the service of the beat, with the result that the rhythm is strengthened and the exhilarative character of the dance is intensified." The number and variety of these dances are so great that only a few can be mentioned here. There are dances in which every muscle is stretched tight, characterized by leaps that seem to be a form of protest against the law of gravity; leap dances, in which the legs are crossed in the air—a primitive *entrechat;* lift dances, in which children are sometimes lifted to promote their growth; slap dances; stride dances; dances in a squatting position; skip dances; knee-lift dances; lunge dances; toe dances; one-legged dances; and many others. In each, not only is something being said—interpersonally or intrapersonally, or to a god, or about a way of life—but the form of each particular dance discloses something about the nature of the culture out of which it came: a culture totemistic and patriarchal, or pastoral, or planter. The dance has a further communicative importance related to every occasion of significance: "for birth, circumcision, the consecration of maidens, marriage, sickness and death, the celebration of chieftains, hunting, war, victory, the conclusion of peace, spring, harvest and pork festivals. Still the themes are limited, for the goal is everywhere the same—life, power, abundance, health" (135).

Yet another distinction is that relating to the **"image or mimetic" dance**, which deals with events or things in nature, and the "imageless or abstract" dance, which is "altogether non-sensory in its origin and in its religious aims. It originates in no perception, it imitates no form and no movement. . . . In contrast with the extraversion of the animal dance it is decidedly a dance of introversion." The image dance "starts with the idea that imitation of gesture and position is sufficient to capture a power and make it useful." That is, if a rain dance in which water is poured from a bowl subsequently brings on a cloudburst, a triumph through the representational has been accomplished. The imageless dance, on the other hand, aims at lifting the body "out of its accustomed corporality, until with the deadening and extinguishing of the outer senses, the subconscious becomes free and increases the spiritual powers . . ." (135). Such dances were—and are—often aimed at interfering with or transcending natural events: the healing of the ill, the betterment of agricultural or human fertility, preparation for battle with another tribe, or to mark such events as marriage or initiation to adulthood.

Of particular interest in the present context is the **"gesture dance,"** which had its beginnings in India thousands of years ago. Such works as the *Nāṭya Śāstra,* written in about the fifth century B. C., and the earlier *Abhinaya Darpaṇa,* the "mirror of gestures," of Nandikéśvara establish "a language of gestures in which the entire representational field of the dramatic dance, according to the theme and emotion expressed, is assigned, down to the last detail, to the various parts of the body. The shaking of the head, for example, signifies negation; looking repeatedly in a certain direction expresses pity, surprise, fear, indifference, coldness, fire, the first moment of drinking, preparation for battle, repulsion, impatience, contemplation of one's own limbs, and a challenge to both sides. Twenty-four such movements of the head are distinguished. But these are only movements of the whole head; four more are allotted expressly to the neck, six to the eyebrows, and twenty-four to the eyes! That no more than fifty-seven positions should be assigned to the hands seems, accordingly, almost too few" (135).

Out of such gestural dances, out of ceremonies and rites, developed the art of **pantomime,** or "dumb-show," a theatrical convention of communication through gesture and expressive action. Historically, its practice in its early states is difficult to separate from certain dance forms, and its relationship to mimicry is rather continuously evident. In at least one place—Athens, in the fourth century B.C.—pantomime had become sufficiently distinct not only to have its professional performers but to be considered seriously enough for the Athenians to collect differing strains of pantomimic art from various sources in tribal cultures.

Classical pantomime not unexpectedly seems to have stressed the notion that movements of all the parts of the body ought to express one definite "idea." And, as it proceeded to divest itself of its earlier religious base and took on more secular colorations, it became a form of popular entertainment; it became "theater"—"a wonderful complex of elements collected from everywhere in the known world" (2). What had begun as a means of communicating the ineffable without the use of language had turned into a means of communication that cut across many languages. Pantomime spread slowly into many countries, though not without attempts at its suppression. The Church, alarmed at pantomime's pagan origins, did its best to do away with it, but its popularity was so great that, instead, Church authorities eventually took it over for their own purposes. In France attempts were made to combine pantomime and ballet. Debureau, the creator of the modern French pantomime, extended the range of pantomime enormously, creating new ones of his own and introducing fresh subtleties and refinements of movement (136). Such great contemporary clowns as the Fratellinis stem from the tradition of Debureau. In England the early pantomime bore down heavily on acrobatic effects, and attempts were made to create a nomenclature of gesture.

The contributions of the United States to pantomime lie chiefly in the **silent motion picture**. With the death of vaudeville, and with the clown tradition carried on only by a handful of men, techniques of wordless gesture and silent action gained a new and incisive impetus. Through the very nature of the medium of the silent movie and the necessity of conveying emotion without the benefit of words, a premium was placed on actors capable of making the utmost of a wink of the eye, a wave of the hand, or a foot aimed at another person's behind. Whereas classical pantomime had dealt with the "single idea," and the Harlequin-Pierrot tradition had dealt with a range of emotions and situations that was scarcely compendious, the silent movie comedians had freedom to range through space and time, to upset the laws not only of motion but of probability and gravity, and consequently to arrive at aspects of the visual that had hitherto been undreamed of. The early innovators and experimentalists in film techniques were quick to realize the essential nature of cinema —that it is, in Cocteau's phrase, "an image-making machine." (29). Through stop action and trick photography and by cutting (montage), and by way of sudden juxtapositions of numerous individual shots, through lap dissolves, superimposition of scenes, double images, and flashbacks, film makers could achieve effects the human eye had never before seen (116). Thoughts could be conveyed visually, and dreams cinematically externalized. The comedians seized upon the new medium in still another way. In molding their cinematic personalities they proclaimed a special faith in the nonverbal: Keaton, frozen-faced, taciturn, noncommittal; Chaplin, the man who is "acted upon"; Harold Lloyd, who escaped vast dangers witlessly; Harry Langdon, withdrawn and woebegone, whose appearance required major efforts on the part of his observers to believe him capable of setting forth a coherent syllable; and the peerless W. C. Fields, whose analogic skills were matched by significant verbal abilities that carried him successfully through the transition to talking films and to later achievements.

The efficacy of **comedians, clowns, and silent movie actors** lies in the projection of ideas and emotions through gesture. Stanislavsky (149), the influential theoretician of acting, admonishes the stage actor, in his first steps toward "working up" a character, not to do so in a studied and programmatic way, but through a search for one encompassing psychological gesture that aims at summing up the character. The use of such a movement not only lays a sort of basic structure for the part, but apparently strengthens the control of the actor over his role as the gesture is repeated. Initial analytic or coldly calculated forays on a role are discouraged, because of their tendency to block acting ability in part or altogether. The actor is encouraged not so much to "live the part" but to produce effects of psychological authenticity through the device of an initial gesture.

The dance, pantomime, mimicry, and acting all have their specific and frequently involved approaches to bodily movement (150). The varieties of action upon which each depends thus constitute a special language capable of statements of an entirely different order from that of words. The work of performers in these fields—the best of whom are not only keen observers of action, but refiners and interpreters—is a source of first importance to the understanding of the larger abstractions by which men of various times and cultures have communicated. Finally, the influence of these interpreters of action upon those who see them

CHARLIE CHAPLIN

3

MASTERS OF FILM PANTOMIME

BUSTER KEATON

HAROLD LLOYD

is unreckoned but undoubtedly considerable in shaping motions, gestures, and behavior in general. Examples are the conscious aping of the postures of cowboy stars on the part of small boys, and the attempts of adolescent girls to handle themselves, from generation to generation, like Mary Pickford or Clara Bow or Ava Gardner. Indeed, there must be few persons of any age who have not, at one time or another, moved, consciously or unconsciously, in step with the image of some actor or actress.

Action Languages

Man has used **action signals** for thousands of years, sometimes as substitutions for verbal signals, sometimes as auxiliary devices for speech. Some have been combined into intricate language systems: the signal fires of the Greeks and Romans, the smoke signals of American Indians, the talking drums of African natives, the signal systems of the navies and merchant marines employing the international code of signals transmitted by semaphore, flag, light, or sound (71). All these systems were introduced because the signals carried farther than the human voice, and messages could thus be relayed quickly over long distances. Not all nonverbal signals, however, were built upon previous linguistic understanding. Gestural language, which contains some seven hundred thousand distinctly different signals, is assumed to have preceded oral speech by close to a million years (118). The North American Indians were among those who developed a systematized and universal sign language of their own (156). In spite of linguistic differences among the various tribes, they could carry on elaborate conversations on any topic. Later, this sign language was adopted by the Boy Scouts, with the intention of enabling members from different countries to communicate with each other at international jamborees.

Perhaps the best example of short-range, visually perceived signaling is the language of the motorist. Driving creates perhaps the only universal situation in which persons are compelled by law to address one another by means of visually perceived signals. Among the **systematized action languages**, many have grown out of specialized vocations. These have developed either because of distance of workers from each other, as among surveyors, or because the human voice may be drowned out by noise, as in the construction industry. The nature of concerts, radio broadcasts, and television shows determines that the instructions of conductors, recording engineers, and producers must be given in gestural terms. Similar considerations apply to hunters stalking their prey, soldiers preparing for surprise attacks, and other persons not wishing to be heard.

Although the systematized action languages are based on prior verbal agreements and merely substitute for human speech, there are other forms of action that serve as codification and that exist quite independently of words. Darwin (33) postulated that certain emotional states are associated with **reflexlike motions**—for example, rage with gritting teeth, or fright with recoiling. His theory—that many of the expressive movements observed in men constitute residuals of lower levels in phylogenetic development—may or may not be correct. The important issue is that, for purposes of communication, people make the assumption that feelings are linked with certain expressive movements and that these movements escape voluntary control. In criminal investigations and in court, this notion is exploited in goading suspects to betray their "real" emotions.

For the communication expert, the issue of whether an action language is innate or based upon prior verbal agreement is less important than the fact that certain actions convey information about the person who performs them. Under the heading of **expressive movements** (3) are included all glandular, vascular, and intestinal manifestations—that is, the movements of the smooth muscles—along with all voluntary and involuntary gestures, including any other purposive, nonverbal actions that have communicative value. Expressive movements are used as a source of information both about the transmitter and about extraorganismic events that may be signified.

In the process of communication through action, the location of the muscles or muscle groups, together with their contractile characteristics, become means of denotation; through combination of location and contraction of one muscle with that of another muscle, physical action becomes a codification system that for certain purposes is superior to words. The fact that such communicative actions may also have immediate adaptive characteristics for the person who performs them in no way reduces their informative value.

The study of silent, **adaptive behavior as a form of language** has only recently come to be emphasized. Traditional preoccupations with such concepts as intention, volition, will, and consciousness led students of human behavior to an overevaluation of the elements of interaction that are explicitly pertinent to communication—spoken and written word, and gesture—although novelists, actors, and dancers have never lost sight of the idea that any silent action might have communicative value. Scientific studies of the communicative aspects of silent action are scarce (102, 126), except for investigations of the social behavior of animals. Since biologists cannot rely upon verbal language to gather their data, they must be skilled at interpreting the action signals of animals. This has been brilliantly accomplished, particularly by Lorenz, Tinbergen, and von Frisch in their studies of geese, wolves, sticklebacks, gulls, bees, and other animals (48, 95, 155).

In contrast to the relative neglect of silent action, considerable attention has been paid to the movements that are used exclusively for communication. These symbolic movements, which in themselves usually cannot gratify any immediate bodily needs, are called **gestures** (63). As is true of the word, the gesture stands for something else; and it is usually employed along with speech (30). Gestures are used to illustrate, to emphasize, to point, to explain, or to interrupt; therefore they cannot be isolated from the verbal components of speech. The understanding of most spoken messages is dependent upon the observation of both verbal and nonverbal codifications, and any isolation of oratorical or conversational gesture is out of the question.

An entirely different kind of action language is found in the **traces that action leaves** on people and things. A ship traveling on the high seas leaves a wake behind; automobile tires make imprints in soft sand; and the path of a jet traveling at high altitude is marked by vapor trails. Footprints, cigarette butts, orange peels, waste paper, ashes, fires, and excrement may mark the trail of the human outdoors. Staircases, doorknobs, benches, shoes, and clothing show marks of wear and tear, to which the human body itself is not immune. Both face and hands—the body parts that are usually kept uncovered—are subject to wear and tear. Callosities form on the hands and feet of those who do manual work or those who walk barefoot. The hands of artisans or of soldiers who handle weapons contrast with the the soft hands of white-collar workers. The **occupational stigmata** from specific physical and mechanical causes that mark workers' hands are innumerable: stains on tanners' or walnut-shellers' hands; the brittle nails of glass polishers; the effects of metal particles on metal-workers' hands; bundle-tiers' grooves; and specially located callosities on banjo-players', flax-spinners', glove-makers', basket-makers', or bakers' hands (125).

Hypertrophy of **muscles** through usage or atrophy because of disuse constitutes another indication of action. Circus acrobats, wrestlers, and boxers show well-developed muscles throughout their bodies. Trombonists and violinists tend to have well-developed arm and shoulder muscles; and workers who use isolated finger movements in their occupations may reveal hypertrophy of single muscles. All actions performed by such workers exercise particular muscle groups, and may serve as occupational marks of recognition. During World War II, Japanese were distinguished from other Asiatics by the fact that they had been wearing sandals: the big toe was spread away from the other toes, whereas the toes of Filipinos, for example, offered no such evidence.

The tonus of the musculature is in part responsible for the flexibility of muscular contraction resulting in movement; conversely, movement is in part responsible for the tonus of the muscles. **Posture** (81) is perhaps the best index of the body's past action, and makes possible the prediction of future bodily performance. Certain standardized postures are conventionally associated with particular occupations and professions. Erect posture is an important part of soldier's training; doormen, butlers, and ushers are similarly expected to meet the world with straight shoulders and protruding chests. Such notions of bearing probably stem from times when the tallest and most erect men had the advantage in hand-to-hand battle. Today, because of different weapons, the advantage may lie with the small man who crouches and stoops. Formerly, the bookkeeper, bending over his books, and elderly persons, affected with arthritis or with a diminishing resilience of their elastic tissues, were supposed to be the embodiment of poor posture and health.

In the study of the traces of action that can be interpreted by other people, and therefore assume the function of language, handwriting—that is, traces of stylus, pen, or pencil left on a surface—carries a particular fascination. The **materials used in the art of writing** belong to two different epochs (69). In the first epoch, characters were engraved with a sharp instrument on hard substances such as metal or stone; in the second, they were written with different liquids or inks on such substances as linen, papyrus, and vellum. The most noteworthy examples of the first period are the engraved records of the Egyptians, for which a fine steel point was probably used. At the time of Moses, and of the Greeks, tablets of wood or lead coated with wax were probably used. The introduction of the use of papyrus to countries beyond the limits of Egypt was the most significant event in the ancient history of writing, comparable in importance to the introduction of printing. In the reign of Ptolemy Lagus, the first Macedonian sovereign of Egypt, papyrus became the substance universally used for literary purposes. It was a small step from papyrus to the development of bark paper, which was known in the sixth century in Europe; further improvements occurred in the ninth century, when cotton was first used to make paper. The first paper mills appeared in the fourteenth century, and eventually led to the production of our present-day varieties of paper.

In ancient times, professional scribes had a monopoly on the production of a brilliantly ornamental calligraphy somewhat similar to contemporary Chinese calligraphy (35); only after the invention of the printing press, which largely obviated the scribes, did **handwriting** as the personal expression of large numbers of people came into prominence. The first extensive treatise on the interpretation of handwriting was published in 1874 by Michon, and thereafter the center of graphology moved from France to Germany, to Switzerland (80), and then on to England and America (137).

The pressure applied in handwriting and the alternating change of flexor and extensor innervation result in an individual patterning that is difficult to disguise, a circumstance that has been widely applied in criminology. Today a considerable number of experts in graphology make a living from interpreting personality through handwriting. Such criteria as regularity, harmony, complexity of forms, spaciousness, speed, pressure, width of tracing, slant, stroke, connecting links, space distribution, and bond or release, though varying slightly from school to school, are almost universally employed. Graphology is an outstanding example of the use of nonverbal cues for the interpretation of an essentially verbal activity.

Body and Appearance as Language

Just as an object, an action, or a word may stand for something else, the human body or parts thereof have been considered to symbolize characteristics of the soul, the mind, or the temperament of the person. From the beginning of recorded history, men have been guided in their judgments by the observation of **facial expression.**

The first treatise on this subject has been rightly or wrongly attributed to Aristotle (5); in ancient times, and especially since the Platonic revival in the thirteenth century, physiognomy has fascinated both charlatans and scientists. Because knowledge of the human psyche is, even in our present era, rudimentary and incomplete, the physiognomists have tended to borrow their concepts from ancient anatomy and physiology. Consequently, it is not surprising to see that Greek physiognomists were linked by theory to the humorologists. Growing out of the cosmology of Empedocles, humoral doctrine maintained that men mirrored nature and thus "contained" the natural world. Blood, with its warm and moist qualities, was a "reflection" of air; phlegm was a "reflection" of water. Characteristics of temperament were ascribed to the humors of the body; the sanguine, melancholic, choleric, and phlegmatic temperaments of Hippocrates formed the backbone of psychological theory for more than two thousand years. The physiognomic diagnosis of these temperaments was partly based upon body structure, considered to be the constitutional-hereditary component, and upon muscular tone, which was thought to be influenced by movement and experience.

The more recent versions of ancient physiognomy and humoral psychology are modern **constitutional psychology and anthropology.** Kretschmer's work (83) still clung to the physique-character parallelism. The leptosome, or asthenic physique, was associated with the schizothymic qualities of introversion, idealism, and formalism; the pyknic physique was related to the cyclothymic qualities of extraversion and realism. In America, Sheldon (145) developed such ideas into a more workable method. His somatotyping consists of taking photographs of subjects from the front, side, and back before a graduated screen. Subsequent ratings of the photographs on a seven-point scale along three coördinates, labeled "endomorphy," "mesomorphy," and "ectomorphy," enabled him to carry out elaborate statistical studies and to define the physique-temperament parallelism in more rigid terms. Sheldon advanced the premise that behavior is a function of structure; he developed psychological counterparts to his physical coördinates, labeling these accordingly "viscerotonia," "somatotonia," and "cerebrotonia"; he applied his methodological and theoretical knowledge to the study of delinquency (146).

The attempts to interpret the body in language terms have not been limited to those who consider the body—or the face—as a whole. Many of the body's parts have been isolated and vested with predictive value. The gypsies' attempts to predict the future on the basis of chiromantics, and more academic attempts to regard the appearance of the hand as the seat of character representation, are but two examples. Wolfe says (165):

> The **hand** as both a tool of learning about the outside world and as an organ of spatial sensibility can be considered the fundamental vehicle of the structure of thought. Spatial differentiation goes with physical as well as mental "balance," and gives to perception the tri-dimensional aspect essential to the orientation of man in the outside world and to its representation in his mind. One can therefore say that the hand as an organ of sensibility assures spatial or tri-dimensional imprints of the outer world in the cortex of the brain.

Similar attempts with other organs include Cherry's *Otyognomy* (28) of 1900, which is charming and naïve in its period assumption that vast insights into character may be read from the human ear.

In these as well as in the older versions of constitutional psychology, there is an underlying desire to systematize the bodily configurations of man. The implicit hypothesis is that the body reflects certain psychological characteristics. If we knew more about such relationships we could make use of them scientifically, much as people do in their daily lives, for purposes of prediction and interaction. The systematizers of the theory of constitutional types (85) are merely attempting to put into scientific language the fact that man, erroneously or judiciously, has always regarded body build, facial expression, and appearance as language.

The fact that novelists frequently describe the appearance of characters and the nature of situations in minute detail relates to the predictive value of **appearance** in human relations. Appearance not only conveys either accurate or false ideas about the bearer of a given physique, but also sets the expectations of an onlooker. The pump-priming capacity of both beauty and ugliness is well known in human relations, in spite of the fact that all historical periods have their own notions of aesthetics. Whether beauty is inherent in the object or is merely a function of the perceiver (54), it is sufficient to point out here that any morphology carrying the stamp of popular or expert appreciation forces the perceiver to take a stand: to acknowledge, refute, or ignore. For example, a beautiful woman asking a favor is likely to receive more spontaneous and speedy service than an unattractive one; people hire, fire, marry and divorce, attract, and reject others on the basis of a compound assessment of both appearance and performance.

The appearance of the human body can be radically changed by particular kinds of **clothing**. The Greek and Roman styles of costume remained fairly constant for centuries, and changes in fashions of dress probably made their appearance in Europe in the fourteenth century (89). Originating at the courts, and spreading later to the population at large, fashions are now promoted not only by Paris *haute couture* but by the mass-producing garment industry in America and elsewhere. A person's identity and taste may be established by apparel, as well as by conformity to the style of the year or the season; clothing, with its capacity for hiding defects in bones and muscles, may be regarded as a particular language in itself (43, 66).

Closely associated with clothing is the personal care of the face, hair, teeth, hands, and legs. In many primitive tribes, status and achievement are indicated by a particular style of **hairdress**. Among Celts, Germans, and Greeks, short hair was a sign of servitude, long hair the sign of a free man. As late as 1945, Frenchmen shaved the hair of woman collaborationists, as both a punishment and a communicative sign of utter disgrace. Both inmates of penitentiaries and military recruits must submit to barber shears as their freedom is restricted. Americans have verbally defined such male "types" as crew-cut and long-hair types. Wigs, which were known in ancient times in Egypt, Greece, and Rome, reappeared prominently at the court of the bald Louis XIII, and in seventeenth- and eighteenth-century Europe were worn by both men and women. Denoting rank and prestige, wigs are still part of the official dress of barristers, judges, the lord chancellor, and the speaker of the house in England.

Since acting is a conscious effort to convey statements to the audience and to elicit certain responses, the language of theatrical costumes and **masks** has a particular communicative significance. On the Victorian stage, for example, black hair indicated the villain, fair hair the hero. Correspondingly, masks were used to indicate such emotions as anger or grief (11). Today, masks are still worn in traditional Japanese and Chinese drama; most native tribes—American Indians, South Sea Islanders, and African Negroes, to mention only a few —use masks in ceremonials, largely because the natural facial expressions of humans are apparently considered insufficient to reproduce the range of effects desired. In modern times, Western Europeans and Americans rarely wear masks except at balls and such celebrations as the Mardi Gras (111). Make-up, however, not only markedly alters the female face, but may communicate a wide range of ideas relating to age, moods, the desire to be desired, professional role, sense of order, time of day, and conventionality. Glasses, which are usually worn because of visual defects, are similarly used to make statements: the horn-rimmed spectacles of the professional man or woman are regarded as trademarks in much the same way as the pince-nez and the monocle.

This brief **review** of object, pictorial, action, and gestural languages may perhaps suffice to point to the extraordinary importance of our nonverbal world. Because reference to this nonverbal world is usually made without verbal elaboration, people are inclined to ignore it. The result is that our educational system, jobs, professions, and ways of assessing personality—particularly in the middle class—are largely geared to the verbal capacities of the individual. But even those who ignore the nonverbal must rely on it to communicate at all. From the range and variety of universally understood nonverbal signals and language systems, it should become more and more apparent that any isolation of any particular aspect of communication is likely to be misleading. To emphasize the nonverbal thus fulfills only one function: to bring our knowledge and skills up to the level of our verbal knowledge and skills. Then—we hope—verbal and nonverbal communication will be treated as a total and inseparable unit.

II MESSAGE THROUGH NONVERBAL ACTION

Incidentally, there are people who seem completely staggered when one talks about nonverbal referential processes—that is, wordless thinking; these people simply seem to have no ability to grasp the idea that a great deal of covert living—living that is not objectively observable but only inferable—can go on without the use of words. The brute fact is, as I see it, that most of living goes on that way. That does not in any sense reduce the enormous importance of the communicative tools—words and gestures.

Harry Stack Sullivan

4. NONVERBAL EXPRESSION

All signals that human beings use to communicate with each other originate in some **physical action** implemented by the contraction of smooth or striped muscles. Speech sounds, for example, are produced through the action of the respiratory muscles as air passes through the larynx and through changes in the positions of the vocal cords, the pharynx, the tongue, and the lips. Verbal signals, however, are accompanied by an enormous variety of nonverbal signals that depend upon the activities of the muscles, glands, skin, or mucosa. Some of these involve involuntary structures—the autonomic nervous system, the smooth muscles, and the endocrine glands; some are mediated through voluntary structures—the central nervous system and the striped muscles affecting tonus, posture, and voluntary movement. Since emotional expression is under both voluntary and involuntary control, it is difficult to hide, particularly when it is intense. Cannon says (25): "There are many **surface manifestations of excitement**. The contraction of blood vessels with resulting pallor, the pouring out of cold sweat,' the stopping of saliva-flow so that the 'tongue cleaves to the roof of the mouth,' the dilation of the pupils, the rising of the hairs, the rapid beating of the heart, the hurried respiration, the trembling and twitching of the muscles, especially those about the lips—all these bodily changes are well recognized accompaniments of pain and great emotional disturbance such as horror, anger, and deep disgust." Changes in skin and muscles inform the observer by visual means, whereas changes in voice patterns impinge upon his ears. In communication both intense and minimal emotional expression may be considered to be a somewhat unintentional message that is not necessarily addressed to any particular person and may not necessarily be purposive. Nonetheless it colors and influences the nature and tone of any message, and often contains explanatory clues about how such a message is meant or is to be taken.

In daily social intercourse the assumption is made that **emotions reflect the inner state of the organism**—not only the more or less hidden thoughts of an individual, but particularly his feelings that are considered to be reflected in his emotional expression (22). In actuality the inner state of the organism may be expressed in a great number of ways, among which nonverbal actions figure prominently. Such ordinary actions as taking off a coat, diving into a pool, or merely walking are as understandable as words to those who see them. Sometimes they enable the onlooker to predict future events more accurately than if he relied upon words alone. And, if he is familiar with the individuals or situations he observes, the possibility of accurate prediction of subsequent behavior becomes even more likely. Both signs of emotion and implemental actions are treated in communication theory as statements addressed **"to whom it may concern."** These statements are not pinpointed for another person's consumption, but they are nonetheless statements. However, since they may not be specifically addressed to another individual, they have been referred to as expressions of the one who speaks or acts.

In contrast to emotional expressions and implemental actions, gestures differ in that they are consciously intended for communicative exchanges and are addressed to particular individuals. However, there are people who gesticulate while talking to themselves, and their actions, when perceived by others, again must be treated as expressions or statements "to whom it may concern."

All expressions of an individual, when perceived by another person, must be interpreted if they are to be understood. Except for the lack of attribution of intention to statements that are regarded as personal or emotional expression, this process of interpretation in no way differs from that used with consciously formulated messages. Thus, in the process of daily living, emotional expression, ordinary adaptive actions, and gestures are treated in somewhat the same manner. In all three, the identification of the **context** of a statement comes first (128). Our language has words for these contexts, and such nouns as "breakfast," "wedding," "cocktail party," "shopping," and "waiting" designate the occasions. After the discovery of an appropriate label for a particular situation, the attempt is made to fit the observed statement to the situation as well as to what is known about the individuals concerned. In pursuit of this aim, the identification of **roles**, including one's own, is necessary. Since the eye is a much faster scanning organ than the ear, and because action is frequently silent, a large part of such initial assessment is carried out visually; if such evaluation were not possible, we would be at a considerable loss in interpreting appropriately, as is evident from the limited and often confusing kind of impressions received in conversations over the telephone.

Photography is capable of recording most of the emotional and action expressions of an individual, although not necessarily in the sense of the nineteenth-century investigators of human behavior. In their accounts of expressive behavior, such pioneers as Wundt (169) and Darwin (33) used sketches and still photographs to illustrate body posture, gesture, and facial expression, but failed altogether to take into account such considerations as those of social context and the role and position of the human observer. It is well to keep in mind that any kind of observation of behavior—with the exception of behavior observed through one-way screens—occurs in two-person or group situations. The very fact of being observed changes, through feedback, the actions and emotions of the observed individual; actions formerly intended for self-consumption then become a statement to others.

As soon as a person is aware of **being observed**, a host of factors begin to influence his behavior; this situation may be visualized by imagining a burglar who is suddenly apprehended by a policeman—in brief, by a human observer. Among the factors that shape the situation are:

Earlier agreements between one and the other, including the implicit agreements embedded in the fact that both participants belong to a culture in which assumptions are made about privacy, property rights, and law

4

ACTION AND COMMUNICATIVE INTENT

Practical implementation as nonintentional
statement

Expressive movements as nonintentional
statements

INTRAPERSONAL ACTION

Practical interpersonal implementation as
statement

Movement as intentional
message to another

INTERPERSONAL ACTION

The social and physical setting that determines the situation: whether they are
   in a home, in a bank, on the street, or perhaps in a car

Familiarity with the observer or the observer's role

The physical distance between the two persons

The presence of a third or still other persons, and whether these are strangers
   or enemies or friends

The expertness of perception and action of the participants

Earlier similar experiences of the participants

The ability to change goals of action suddenly

The ability to initiate appropriate measures to deal with the new situation

In line with the above, some of the pictures in this book document the pleasure or surprise of people when they were aware of being photographed; some even suggest the change that took place when the presence of the photographer was noticed. Some people even took the photographer's presence in their stride—with an awareness that they were perceived but without any major change in their behavior.

In communication, consequently, **distinctions cannot be made between** the adaptive **actions** that implement homeostatic needs and communicative actions that increase a person's knowledge or convey information to others or achieve a calculated effect. Although assumptions are continually being made that clear-cut lines of demarcation exist between unintentional expression on one hand and intentional communication on the other, such lines of demarcation are impossible to maintain scientifically. Not infrequently it can be observed that silent actions implemented through contractions of the smooth or striped muscles can be highly informative whereas statements made through words remain inconsequential or are hardly noticed. Conversely, the usage of words can be so charged that these sounds are frequently confused with physical acts of protection or violence. Replacing the older distinctions between involuntary expression and intentional statement, we have today come to realize that any form of action, whether verbal or nonverbal, has communicative function. As soon as another person interprets a signal with some degree of accuracy, it must be codified in terms that qualify as language.

5. THE INFORMATIVE VALUE OF MOVEMENT

Human movements are determined by biological and experiential factors. The structure of the bones, joints, and muscles; the age of an individual; his height and weight; and a host of other constitutional factors—all determine more than anything else the extent, duration, and speed of the movements a person can make. With this knowledge of physical laws and of biological limitations, any observer attempts to derive from the observation of movements information about the other person. He scans the possibilities, and perhaps marks the other's motions as being influenced by climate, emotions, physical circumstances, disease, or the impact of the actions of still other people.

In the course of such **preliminary and crude assessments** of motion, certain cues are particularly helpful. Evaluation of movement is based principally upon the determination of the point of origin, the point of destination, the direction, and the speed of the moving organism or object. Sometimes the path that the object leaves behind is likewise highly informative. In order to determine the **point of origin**, the eye attempts to trace the moving object back to its point of origin. Apparently the knowledge of the point of origin of a moving object or organism enables the onlooker more accurately to predict the nature of the subsequent events, and also to assess the possible impact of its motion. But the mere identification of a point of origin is often insufficient; the concerned observer tries to follow the movement of an object, person, or animal through space to its **point of destination**. The more he knows about any completed movement cycle, the more he is capable of predicting future action. Once the points of origin and destination are determined, the **direction** of the movement may be established. When an observer is unable to make out both the point of origin and the point of destination, he must be content with information about one fixed point and the direction a moving object or person came from or is headed for.

Human beings react with apprehension to certain movements when they do not know the point of origin, the point of destination, or the direction. For example, if a pedestrian sees a lady's purse emerge from a window and fall to the street, his expected reaction will probably be one of alarm or apprehension; if, however, he sees the person who dropped the purse, he is in a better position to evaluate the situation. Similarly, in warfare, enemy fire from a well-known entrenched position is far less terrifying than the shots of a sniper whose location is unknown. A mother who sees her children leave the house wants to know where they are going; if they announce a definite destination, the mother may not be worried. **Speed** is usually assessed in relationship to the prevailing tempo. Something that moves

Material

Climatic

Biological

Social

THE POINTS OF ORIGIN AND DESTINATION DETERMINE THE DIRECTION OF ACTION

Point of origin

Point of destination

Point of destination as new point of origin

slowly relative to the time scale of the observer is ordinarily considered less dangerous than something that moves more swiftly. Animals and children, in particular, are afraid when movements are so fast that they can scarcely perceive them.

Brief glimpses of persons in action, or of still pictures of these persons in action, enable the observer to make inferences about the speed of movement. Persons sitting, leaning, standing, or lying down hold their limbs in positions that preclude the possibility of fast action. Persons walking or moving slowly or at moderate rates of speed keep their bodies perfectly in balance; such a balance, as recorded by the camera, is inferred by the observer to stand for moderate speed. Persons running or moving at a fast rate of speed appear in still pictures to be in positions of disequilibrium, which the observer interprets as representing fast movement (6).

The nature of the **pathway** that a moving object produces may often have highly significant communicative value. An automobile may proceed in a straight line or may weave in and out of traffic. A drunk may sway, flounder, or stagger from one side to another. Often the informative value is conveyed principally by those body parts that move the most and those that move the least. Sometimes the path of motion and information about the moving parts can be read from tracks or traces of action. For example, a wound may be sharp or jagged, informing a surgeon about the nature of the offending instument, or a streak of paint on an automobile fender may help in locating a hit-and-run driver.

Occasionally the observation of movement must be reconstructed as extending into the past or predicted in terms of the future. **Inferences** of this sort are made continually. We are so accustomed to supplementing social situations with inferences that the sight of a woman pushing a baby carriage automatically triggers the assumption that a baby is in it, even when we cannot see the baby; when persons in a crowd stare in one direction, we spontaneously turn our gaze in the same direction and are curious to find out what it is they are looking at.

Consciously or unconsciously, most people attempt to predict whether or not they may become **personally involved** in social or physical actions that are in progress. We all determine quickly and rapidly whether or not we are going to be in the path of a flying object, a running dog, or an oncoming vehicle. Then we assess the movement according to its directional character, keeping our own position in mind. Assessment of motion is chiefly in terms of whether it is toward a known point, or toward or away from us. In addition, we watch over-all configurations of **mass movement** in order to predict our possible progress toward a goal. Most of us know the frustrating experience of being in a hurry only to be blocked by a crowd of people, who may emerge from a central place and spread in all directions—for example, at the end of a ball game. The path of motion may be conflicting —for example, two lines of people crossing each other and creating confusion at a point of intersection. Movement may be parallel as with marching soldiers, or converging as with people going to church. Movement may be along horizontal or vertical lines, or may occur in frontal or sagittal planes vis-à-vis the observer. Accurate estimates of these constellations help individuals in eventually reaching their desired destinations.

Not only details in the execution of movement, but the evaluation of an action with reference to other actions—actually carried out or merely postulated as a possibility—have informative value. For example, when one person observes another lighting a cigarette, he may place a variety of **interpretations** on this action. With whatever ideas he may have

BODY POSITION INDICATES SPEED OF MOVEMENT

Idling

Low gear

Intermediate

In high

Who or what are they looking at?

INFERENCE OF MISSING PART
WHO OR WHAT?

Who or what is in the buggy?

What's on the other side of the fence?

Emphasis on events to come

Emphasis on past events

Simultaneous emphasis on past, present, and future events

about personality and behavior, he may interpret such an action as conveying merely that the smoker needed oral gratification and that he reached for a cigarette. Action may be thus interpreted as simply satisfying a personal need. Under particular circumstances, however, the observer might ask: "Why is he lighting a cigarette when he knows that I dislike smoke? Is he either inconsiderate or overtly hostile?" Such an interpretation is not reached with considerations of bodily needs in mind, but in terms of an interpersonal situation. The identification of the label of an action combined with information about details of movement and supplemented with speculations about a person's intentions, needs, and motivations thus form the basic material upon which interpretation and assessment of action are built. Such multiple considerations are constantly present in the evaluation of action, contributing significantly to both the understanding and the confusion existing in the communicative process. Because of the great range of possibilities in the interpretation of action, the conscious exploitation of this circumstance is the foremost instrument of concealment and deceit. No one is more keenly aware of this fact than the military strategist or the politician.

6. PEOPLE ALONE

Before individuals can communicate or interpret complex messages, they must identify each other, in even a rough or makeshift way. Thus everyone has a certain **identity**, known to himself and to others, that for all practical purposes remains stable regardless of the social situation in which he participates. This identity expresses itself in physical appearance, movements, and speech patterns. The total appearance of a person furnishes information for initial and tentative assignment of identities and roles; age, sex, body build, clothing—even temperament and intelligence—all furnish helpful clues. Since appearance, body detail, and movement are usually interpreted and assessed in terms of total configurations, logical categorization of detailed factors makes little sense; evaluated as a unit, however, these factors have unquestionable problem-solving properties. Actually, all the signs of body language are mere modifiers of action language. Intuitively, most people interpret action as the principal carrier of information, and make use of additional physical signs merely to amplify and correct the impressions conveyed through bodily movement.

Since people are anatomically and physiologically more alike than different, this circumstance lends itself to comparative and **empathic assessment**. From knowledge of and experience with his own body, one person is capable of inferring another's sensations or judging the condition of the latter's organism. Sometimes movements carried out by particular muscle groups or pointing toward special body areas stand out with arresting significance. For example, most men have at one time or another experienced the sensation of having their trousers slip down, and most women are familiar with the annoyance of a slipping shoulder strap. Those who wear glasses know how they are cleaned; those who use books know how they are carried; and everyone pays attention to cues involved in such activities as tying shoelaces, smoothing the hair, and adjusting garments for purposes of evaluating others on the basis of their own performance of such tasks. The most commonplace activities are the easiest to interpret. Such a widespread habit as smoking and the activities connected with it lend themselves particularly to such interpretation. Subsequently, moving from details to larger Gestalten, and judging from experiences with his own and other social groups, one person is capable of placing another, on the basis of clothing or personal adornment, into the latter's probable position in society.

Foremost among the body parts that have communicative value is the face. **Facial expression** is capable of indicating a wide variety of emotional states about which words can only give rough hints; it is in part dictated by muscular development, in part by the appear-

Infant as sunbather

Workman

Pedestrian as reader

Bobby-soxers

Angry embarrassment

WHAT CHILDREN'S FACES CAN EXPRESS

Self-protection and fear

Phlegmatic disdain

Delight

Dour expectations

Grim fascination

BODY DETAIL CAN BE INFORMATIVE

A firm grip on reading matter

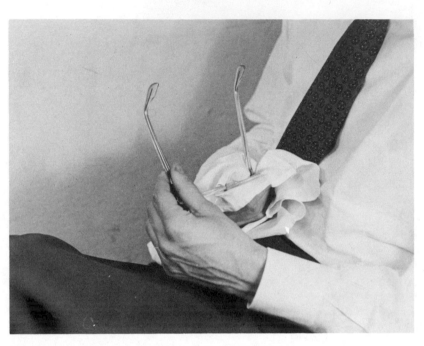

Cleaning glasses as a familiar task

A snug collar facilitates a coquettish pose

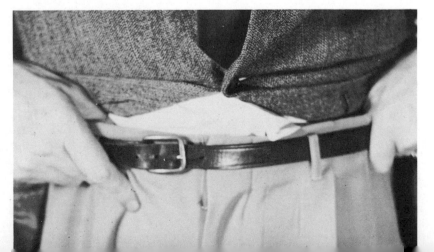

Casualness as a way of life

INDIVIDUAL DIFFERENCES IN SMOKING

WHEN POSTURE REFLECTS MOODS AND ATTITUDES

Expectant

Restful

Meditative

Curious

Self-assured

15
WHEN INTRAPERSONAL GESTURE BECOMES INTERPERSONALLY INFORMATIVE

Reflective scratch

Actual itch

A concerned drag

Apprehensive sucking

A swallow as a stimulus for others

ance of the skin, and in part by the bony structure of the skull. Persons who habitually pull down the corners of their mouths are believed to be expressing contempt. Persons who lift the corners of their mouths are regarded as being good-natured. All cartoonists are familiar with the device of drawing the mouth as an up-or-down semicircle; if they wish to produce the effect of a tight-lipped person, they use a straight line. Lifting one corner of the mouth and pulling it to the side has been associated with feelings of inferiority; the mouth in the middle position, with feelings of security. The muscles of mastication, when habitually contracted, give an appearance of pugnaciousness; the habitual wrinkling of the forehead is considered a mark of seriousness and concern. The interpretation of such expressive movements of the face is a universal experience; when the muscles are used excessively and remain in a semicontracted position, they become monuments of personality structure.

Emotional expression appears most spectacularly when verbal communication fails altogether. The inability to use words occurs when people are overwhelmed by anger, anxiety, fear, or shame. In spite of the incoherent nature of the things they say on such occasions, or the inability to speak at all, others can still understand the implications of their actions. Human cries of fear and the kind of trembling associated with anxiety are correctly interpreted anywhere in the world, and the appearance of tears is universally regarded as a sign of tension release attributed to states of pleasure, pain, or grief. Hence the chief function of emotional expression is that of a universal and international emergency language. When people are alarmed, fatigued, furious, afraid, apprehensive, or embarrassed, others assess them primarily on the basis of those cues that indicate intensity of stimulation and the tolerance limits of the organism. When a mother hears her child crying, she automatically makes a distinction between a feeble whimper or a high-pitched cry, knowing that each sound quality stands for a particular feeling. Such cues of intensity, periodicity, and crescendo and diminuendo—which denote changes in time and are so characteristic of living processes—are impossible to represent verbally; even such a gifted experimentalist in poetry as E. E. Cummings, making use of radical typographical innovations, has been able only to suggest their approximations (31).

Facial expression performs an additional function in that it is interpreted as a **metacommunicative instruction** accompanying verbal messages. When emotional modulations are harmonious and subdued, they are interpreted merely as verbal modifiers; when emotional modulation gathers in intensity, its signs cease to serve predicate functions and are regarded as having become the subject matter itself. Then the intensity of the emotions becomes a signal to onlookers to minimize verbal statements and to regard the situation in the light of emergency.

Still photography has serious limitations in recording emotional modulation and states of emotional emergency; it cannot deal with changes over a period of time, and in the world of being, time and space are inseparable. However, muscular contractions leave their imprints on the skin and the skeletal system, permitting at least some inferences—from **posture** and facial expression—not only about what is happening at the moment but also about what has happened in the past. In general, modulations of facial expression bear more particularly upon momentary experience—a sudden smile, for example—whereas body posture seems to reflect more fixed attitudes and generalized moods.

Facial expression and posture—even the most minute contractions of isolated muscle groups—may be intended either for communicative purposes or for serving personal bodily needs. Such habits as fidgeting, scratching, biting the fingernails, grinding the teeth, or smoothing the eyebrows may have no communicative intent. They are nonetheless interpreted by others, who in turn make inferences about the personalities and temperaments of those who perform them.

When people are alone, they frequently behave as if they were in company; and when in company, they often behave as if they were alone. Although it must be taken for granted that certain individuals behave differently when alone and when with others, the conclusion seems inevitable that the human being as a social animal almost always behaves as if he were in a social situation and in a communicative context. At least for the scientific observer this seems a safe assumption to make. More often than not, it will minimize those errors that were made when the human being was assumed to be a solitary person who was only rarely and intentionally involved in a communicative situation.

7. THE ROLE OF CONTEXT IN THE INTERPRETATION OF ACTION

The unity of the thirteenth century was contrasted by Henry Adams (1) with twentieth-century multiplicity. It may well be that our contemporary concern with social structure and interpersonal relations should be regarded as an attempt to bring some order into the complexities and discrepancies of modern life. Today almost everyone becomes involved in undesired and often changing roles, and many must carry on an incessant struggle for identity. The fluidity of modern life, with its reduction of the personal, almost forces individuals to use functional concepts related to the identification of social situations and social roles. These concepts help the individual to establish a temporary operational definition of the identity of the participants, thus facilitating initial interaction.

The recognition of **roles** is implemented through the perception and interpretation of a variety of strategic cues. The speediest assignment of a role becomes possible when custom or circumstance determines the use of uniforms and one person is able to address another as "Officer," "Waiter," "Nurse," or "Sergeant." Roles may be indicated also through material objects; tools, implements, and machines sometimes identify such persons as welders, musicians, or brakemen. Sometimes a variety of cues throws light on the identification of members of particular trades—when uniforms, props, movements, and even language characteristics contribute to identification. Usually, however, such identification is far more complex, since any one person may fulfill multiple roles at the same time—roles defined in terms of age, sex, occupation, family position, citizenship—and may shift through a number of such transient roles as those of a pedestrian, passenger, spectator, or consumer. The cues singled out and fixed upon are also determined not only by the subjective needs and expectations of the participants but by the total context of the situation. For example, a waiter is not—needless to say—addressed as "Waiter" when he is in any other than his professional context.

Roles are **multipolar phenomena** regulating the communication systems of two or more persons. In some situations one pole of the role system is specified and the other is fluid. The concept of role of a traffic officer fixes his relationship to those he directs, whereas the drivers and pedestrians have more latitude of action and the possibility of changing their own roles. Such asymmetries are less common in two-person situations where the reciprocal roles of mother and child, husband and wife, or pilot and navigator are more rigidly defined. Two-person relationships are a function of the context in which they occur, and may be superseded or crisscrossed by other interpersonal relations. In nonverbal communication,

Bootblack: by activity
and background

Student or professional:
by portfolio

Shopper: by prop

Postman: by uniform

17

IDENTIFICATION OF TWO-PERSON RELATIONSHIPS

PALS
Cues of relationship derived from parallel position and shared seating accomodations

MOTHER-CHILD RELATIONSHIP
Cues derived from age, size, sex, and expressive movements

A PAIR
Cues of relationship derived from expressive movement

GROUP IDENTIFIED BY BACKGROUND AND SPACING

Working-class men

Middle-class women

STATUS IDENTIFIED BY CLOTHING

Unrelated individuals forming a group
waiting to cross.

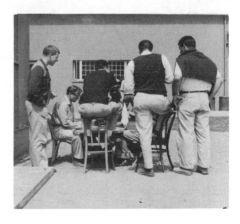

A "group" actually composed
of two groups—card players
and kibitzers

IDENTIFICATION THROUGH ASSOCIATION AND ACTIVITY

THE STATUS OF INDIVIDUALS IN GROUPS

Status through sex appeal

Status through headgear

Status contrast marked by garb and posture

Status through mount and uniform

Priority takes precedence over other status considerations

THE IDENTIFICATION OF SOCIAL SITUATIONS

SERVICE SITUATION
Cues derived from background,
equipment, costume, and posture

PLAY SITUATION
Cues derived from prop, age, and activity

CONVERSATIONAL SITUATION
Cues derived from grouping and
gestures

FAMILY SITUATION
Cues derived from age, sex, grouping,
and the ways in which the participants
face each other

the interpretation of mutual roles serves the purpose of clarifying the verbal, gestural, and action messages that people consciously convey to each other—hence, roles are also **meta-communicative statements**. Those who are quick to recognize roles and are aware of the shifting nature of roles are at an advantage in dealing with social situations. The number of misunderstandings that occur through a failure to recognize a change in role is staggering. For example, at one moment a man may talk and act as a father, in the next in his capacity as a husband, and then again as a tennis player. Others who participate in the conversation may or may not follow these shifts with comprehension. It is scarcely accidental that some of the most worldly and discerning of novelists—for example, Henry James, Marcel Proust, Ford Madox Ford, Gustave Flaubert, Thomas Mann, E. M. Forster, Conrad Aiken, and F. Scott Fitzgerald—are continuously and even obsessively preoccupied with the concept of role and its importance in shaping the incongruities, ironies, and tragedies of human existence. James' *The Sacred Fount* (73) takes the awareness of role as its subject matter almost with a vengeance, as does Flaubert's *Bouvard and Pécuchet* (42); its significance for individual representatives of two cultures is extremely marked in Forster's *A Passage to India* (44).

Relationships as defined through roles are not limited to individuals, but are meaningful in identifying **groups** vis-à-vis each other—for example, spectators and players, labor and management, and civilians and soldiers. In such circumstances individual identity is submerged and persons are regarded as members of large organizations. Since large groups rarely interact with each other—except perhaps in time of war—spokesmen for each group transact business in the name of their organizations. Upon the skillful implementation of shifting roles at such levels may depend strikes, trade treaties, international tension, and possibly war.

A particular kind of role is expressed through the symbols of **status and prestige.** Society is vertically stratified, and whatever names are used to denote prestige groups and social classes, the identification marks of status differences are known and recognized. In one culture, they may distinguish peasant from nobleman or party member from nonmember; in our culture, they are the signs that identify lower, middle, and upper classes. Although people congregate socially in separate groups, by necessity they must cross class boundaries as well. The manager of a factory deals with his employees, the battalion commander "mixes" with his soldiers while on duty, and the teacher as a matter of course interacts with his students. Although such confrontations continually occur, status characteristics are carefully preserved and identified by dress or uniform or are conveyed by marks of age, sex, skill, or wealth. Just as roles are communicative statements without which verbal communication as we know it would be impossible, symbols of status explain aspects of power and prestige—imaginary or real—that an individual possesses or wishes to suggest he may possess.

In the practice of communication, we are continually assessing our material surroundings, making attempts at identifying others and their roles, their status, and their group membership in order to arrive at a kind of diagnosis that will combine all these features into an integral pattern: the **social situation.** In the truest sense, it is the social situation that determines the context and nature of any communicative exchange. It would be unthinkable for anyone to disrobe in the middle of Park Avenue, even though wearing a bathing suit, but such an activity would pass without a glance at Coney Island. Such a strict definition of behavior takes into account not only implementations but the kind and style of verbal com-

THE RULES OF ACTION

Run, push, and hold on

Keep your balance

MATERIALLY DETERMINED RULES OF ACTION

Sit down and be quiet

Group yourselves in a line

SOCIALLY DETERMINED RULES OF ACTION

RULES IMPROVISED

SITUATIONS SUPERSEDING EACH OTHER

ACCOMPANIMENT
Itch as intermezzo

IMPROVISATION
Lunch takes precedence over office
etiquette

EMERGENCY
Fire takes precedence over propriety

ROUTINE DIVERGENCE
Unloading takes precedence over departure

munication as well. Such settings as night clubs, conference rooms, Turkish baths, and vestry rooms rigidly define what may or may not be said or done.

Once a social situation has been identified, persons automatically apply **rules** of behavior they feel to be pertinent. These rules may be determined in part by the action itself, particularly when the application of inappropriate rules might result in personal inconvenience or even injury or death. On other occasions misinterpretation or violation of rules may bring about reprimands, social ostracism, or civil censure. However, personal survival would not be possible if we could not occasionally break, modify, or improvise rules. This is particularly true when one social situation merges into another.

Just as scientists in modern field theory have distinguished between field forces—that is, the parameters of the system—and variables that pertain to the action itself, so do we all distinguish between social context and communicative action. Whereas the parameters of a communicative situation are defined through physical and social context, roles, and rules, the process under observation is defined by the activity of signaling. The parameters thus become interpretive devices—that is, metacommunicative devices—for the understanding of the signals.

8. PEOPLE TOGETHER

As our society is ordered, verbal language is indispensable. Without numbers and words, the cumulative body of knowledge of mankind could not have been codified. Consequently the practice in higher educational procedure has been to spend some ten to twenty years indoctrinating the young in specific ways of reading, writing, speaking, and calculating. Unhappily, however, our verbal-digital education is not paralleled by a corresponding regard for training along nonverbal, analogic lines. Thus we continue to produce—as though completely to reverse the views of the Renaissance—more and more narrowly oriented human beings as well as increasing numbers of quasi schizophrenics, capable of grappling with the most complicated mathematical and technological problems but with no real understanding of the actions of human beings, their emotional expression, or even of gesture—all of which are so necessary for the understanding of speech.

Gesture is language. Though gestures are, of course, determined by the way the human body is constructed, even those gestures that border on reflexes are necessarily elaborated in an interpersonal and social context. As a result, expressions of amazement, desperation, resignation, pride, anger, anxiety, and pleasure are similar in certain respects in all countries and cultures; in other respects the understanding of their meaning is dependent upon familiarity with the entire communication system of a given culture. Each individual, through the gestures he chooses to make and the way in which he makes them, adds an idiosyncratic note that may have particular communicative significance only to close acquaintances.

The scientific approach to gesture involves first of all an analysis of movements in their **spatiotemporal characteristics.** Efron (36), one of the few investigators to have made a close study of the subject, has concluded that the formal analysis of gestures should include a spatiotemporal description in terms of the body parts involved, the radius of the moving parts, the type and form of motion (elliptical, lineal, sinuous), the plane in which the action is carried out (frontal, sagittal), the speed of movement, the transfer of gestures from one part of the body to another, the unilaterality or bilaterality of the gesture, and the involvement of large or small muscles.

A second scientific approach is found in an analysis of the **linguistic aspects** of gesture. Certain gestures may be used as substitutes for words—for example, the "V for Victory" sign, later converted by Winston Churchill into a personal signal of recognition and understanding. Here the understanding of the gesture is based on earlier agreement. More often than not, however, gestures are not a substitution for, but an accompaniment to, words.

GESTURES AS SUBSTITUTES FOR WORDS

Bye-bye

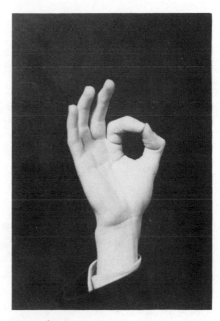

Just right

Louder, please

Over there

NONVERBAL ACCOMPANIMENTS OF
VERBAL COMMUNICATION

Directional illustration

Emphasis

Shared focus of attention

The attempt to catch another's gaze

The physical embodiment of secret conversation

Get on and off where congestion is least

Two-way traffic on one-way streets

Left hand up means right-hand turn

As though for livestock

The skittish demand a special etiquette

COOPERATION AND NONVERBAL COMMUNICATION

Individual action imitated

Individual action pooled

Individual action complemented

Coöperation between old and young

Action integrated into teamwork

Unsolicited courtesy

INTERPERSONAL DISTANCE

Transaction at arm's length

Play at close quarters

Closeness and touch can convey affection

An unrelated pair

One and a couple

Gestures may express both appreciation and sensuousness, as when two hands are curved in the air to suggest an attractive female shape; or they may express the impact of an action upon the body, as in a grimace at the thought of some revolting food. Conversely, gestures may be used also as devices of punctuation, conveying such abstract concepts as rhythm, timing, acceleration, or emphasis. Accordingly, analytic classifications have been used by the authors of oratorical textbooks (7), who have even suggested that the compilation of a dictionary of gestures could be meaningful (8). In the same vein, others have attempted to analyze period gesture solely in terms of evidence from novels, plays, and poems (160). However, such attempts to break down gestures into emphasizing, pointing, explicative, interruptive, and reinforcing devices represent an artificial approach, and neglect the fact that gesture is inseparably linked to other elements of communication.

The scope of modern civilization shapes gesture, and many men adapt gesturally to their life with **machines**. Many kinds of work, such as radio production, surveying, aviation, and the construction industry, have specific gestural languages all their own, either because engine noise drowns out the human voice or because the human voice does not carry far enough. Depending upon the nature of the social situation, gestures may be employed because the use of the voice would constitute interference, as in hunting, military ambush, or during musical performances. In situations involving rapid motion, gestures become mandatory because words cannot be understood. Thus the language of traffic is based almost entirely upon nonverbal signals. Gestures are essential where verbalization is impossible: where linguistic barriers exist or when difficulties of hearing prevail. Gestures are often used when particular kinds of verbal expression would be considered obscene or in bad taste.

So much for gesture. There are many situations, however, in which particular statements are made by way of movements that have no intentional language function. Football players watch each other and their adaptive movements intently, ostensibly concerned with the manipulation of the ball, but actually for purposes of determining messages relating to present and future action. Communication of this sort, through **adaptive action,** is the basis of all coöperative activity, ranging from the closely timed movements of circus acrobats to the casual movements of encounters on the street.

When someone wishes to appraise others in terms of friendliness or hospitality, one of his major clues is the physical distance maintained. This may range from actual touch to various spans of distance, indicating familiarity or strangeness, or intimacy or remoteness. Physical distance, in turn, is determined by the habits of the participants. Someone who gesticulates within a certain radius, for example, keeps his listeners at arm's length or less; one who seems about to explode emotionally is kept at a distance by others. Invitations to decrease or increase distance are often extended visually. Some, through a skillful exposure of skin, invite touch; others, because of an overly immaculate countenance, exert a forbidding influence. Such visual cues thus control social situations through an appeal to either the proximity or the distance receivers.

All coöperative activities begin with the acknowledgment of the participants' **perception of each other;** this marks the opening signal for subsequent communicative exchanges. The perception of perception is characterized by an alteration of the direction of gaze, by change of body position, by signs of pleasure or annoyance—all of which may indicate, through a break in the continuity of previous activity, that a new situation is in the making.

Mutual perception

Chain of perception: Spectators
watch players; passers-by watch
spectators

The pleasure of being photographed

Curious approach

The pleasure of getting closer

The alarm at another's departure

ASSISTANCE AND SUPPORT

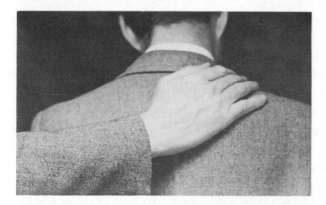

Gesture of moral support

Proffered light

The pleasure of feeding and being fed

Paternal consolation: squatting down

Maternal consolation: picking up and holding tight

As all hunters are aware, the animal's signal of having perceived danger is to interrupt whatever it was doing, freeze momentarily, and then proceed to defensive action or escape. Similar criteria apply to cues involved in interpersonal **leave-takings** and the disbanding of groups. In spontaneous group formation, people ordinarily face each other when talking; when taking leave of each other on the street, they turn their ventral sides away from each other. This is done gradually by taking a few steps backward, and only after intermediary signals of saying goodbye do they walk directly away from each other (133).

In interpersonal meeting, gesture and action tend to have a more **mandatory function;** they direct or shape the other person's behavior, whereas words serve a more explanatory function. When a mother consoles her child, her touch is gentle while her words are aimed at clarifying the nature of the trouble. Gestures may express "here," "there," or "nowhere." Movements of a host offering his guest a seat may indicate precisely in which chair he wishes the guest to sit. The posture of the housewife in her doorway is a strong indication to a salesman as to whether he is going to be allowed to enter or not.

By means of the duality of verbal and nonverbal communication, the human being is able to create **impressions based upon differences** between the things he says in words and the things he communicates through action. He may, for example, say, "I love you, darling," at the same moment that he is digging his fingernails into the palm of his hand. Freud's contribution in emphasizing the importance of supposedly insignificant slips in this area of communication revealed the fact that words can be diametrically opposed to what is expressed through action or gesture (46). Depending upon personality and age, an individual may either respond selectively to action and gesture—the nonverbal components of language—or reply selectively to the verbal elements of language; finally, and this under optimal conditions, he may attempt to integrate the verbal and the nonverbal components into a whole, thus trying more fully to interpret the message under consideration. In social intercourse, the person who can derive useful information from apparent contradictions—resulting from a comparison of the various means of codification—has the advantage over others. The person who manages apparent contradictions by disregarding part of the message—those statements that are codified in different terms—loses much information, is likely to misinterpret the message, and is generally less capable of successful communication.

III MESSAGE THROUGH OBJECT AND PICTURE

To be at all critically, or as we have been fond of calling it, analytically, minded—over and beyond an inherent love of the general many-colored picture of things—is to be subject to the superstition that objects and places, coherently grouped, disposed for human use and addressed to it, must have a sense of their own . . . to give out, that is, to the participant at once so interested and so detached as to be moved to a report of the matter.

Henry James

9. CODIFICATION IN MATERIAL TERMS

Signaling by means of word, gesture, or other action by no means exhausts the possibilities of communication; on the contrary, a whole series of situations exists in which people influence, guide, and direct each other by means of signals that are embedded in the material environment. Objects as systems of codification are used pervasively in every walk of life—in business and at home, ranging from household gadgets to articles of furniture. Architectural style, interior decoration, and lighting conditions, for example, also play significant parts in communication. Thus there is little doubt that the nonverbal and often unconscious exchange of messages codified in material terms fulfills all the criteria of language; for brevity's sake, we shall subsequently refer to it as **object language**.

The language of objects is outspokenly used in the world of trade, where shop windows and commercial exhibits are arranged with the undisguised purpose of attracting customers. Rarely if ever does a verbal description achieve the same effect as an exhibit of merchandise; no merchant would attempt to influence his customers through the display and arrangement of things if it were not for the fact that the success of such nonverbal methods can be evaluated in terms of dollars and cents. In this field, consequently, no conjecture is involved. The intent to influence and sell is unconcealed. And the fact that objects on display are bought would indicate that the desired effect is frequently achieved. Objects for commercial display, as they appear in showcases and store windows, usually convey brief and simple statements; in private homes, statements through objects become more complex and the intentions of the owners far less open and transparent.

The effects that objects achieve in terms of their communicative value are dependent not only upon arrangement but also upon variations of **material, shape, and surface**. Any material evokes tactile and thermal images—of smoothness, roughness, hardness, softness, coldness, and warmth. Wood, metal, brick, and textiles produce a variety of anticipations of touch sensations. Wood against wood, metal against brick, a stiffened fabric against a soft and pliable one—all set up "chords" of tactile images that often produce sharp and immediate physical and emotional reactions. Metal may be highly polished or finished with a dull patina; containers may be opaque, translucent, or transparent. Surfaces—whether raised, carved, rough, or smooth—when exposed to light reflections, are likely not only to express the moods of those who shaped them, but also to suggest such subtle and abstract matters as interpenetration or merely the simple adjoining of boundaries.

Statement through single object

Statement through repetition

Statement through framed
arrangement

Textile

Wood

Paper

Iron

ORDER AND DISORDER

Conventional order

Conventional disorder

Unconventional order

Accident

HOW OBJECTS ARE COMBINED INTO A WHOLE

Whole through central figure

Whole through frame

Unconcern with whole: unrelated objects together

Placement of objects to satisfy impression of whole

Neglect of whole: displaced object

Once an object exists, it may be used in a variety of ways. A trash receptacle can be identified by its design, and a hole in its top instructs, "Put your trash through this opening." The one in Plate 31 announces, through its weathered state, some idea of its age and use; the handles indicate that it can be lifted, carried, and tossed. The **arrangement** of similarly shaped objects reinforces or attenuates the impression made by the single object. Several rounded and hollow articles enhance the impression of containment and maneuverability. For example, the display of stockings, mounted on several models of legs cut off below the knee, puts over the idea of stockings, legs, quality, diversity, and whatever other connotations the spectator wishes to assign to it. Form is conveyed not only through the shape of the individual object, but also by way of the character of a layout. Buttons, for example, framed in ordered rows as if they were collector's items, suggest plentiful supply, ready availability, specialization; and to some they may hold the promise of expert service.

Although standardization has limited expression through personal craftsmanship, an object can nonetheless be connected with the personality of its maker; or it can be connected with its owner; or a combination of objects may be linked to the person who made the arrangement. The selection of objects and the nature of their grouping constitute nonverbal expressions of thoughts, needs, conditions, or emotions. Thus, when people shape their surroundings, they introduce man-made **order**. Such arrangements may follow a rigid geometrical order based on symmetry or repetition from which randomness is carefully excluded. In other arrangements, even in carefully arranged display, order may occasionally be disturbed through true accident; an object or a carton of food may move from its place and remain where it fell. Between these extremes are several other possibilities. A comfortable state of informality may be achieved by throwing cushions customarily used outdoors into a wicker basket in the living room; a shop may hint at its readiness to deliver goods by displaying flowers as though they had been casually tossed into the window.

Order implies the notion of arrangement of parts into a **whole**. When a person has to deal with thousands of separate items, whether they are objects or pieces of information, his problem is one of simplification. In object language the arrangement of many small items into a whole achieves brevity and compactness of expression, just as abstraction unites many subordinate thoughts into an over-all idea. A variety of methods may be used to achieve such a whole.

In Plate 34 the barber supply house displays cosmetics in a window outlined by a white brick frame, as though in answer to a felt need for geometrical enclosure, setting off the place of business from adjoining stores. Around a play on words—"The Knight before Christmas" —a decorator has loaded a suit of armor with diversified presents, thus achieving unity in spite of variety. On a drop-leaf desk, figurines are arranged into a formal whole at the expense of practicality; turning the desk into a showcase necessitates unusual preparations before anyone can work there. There are those who do not care about producing an impression of unity. When a merchant puts model airplanes in his window, for whatever reasons he may have, the onlooker has difficulties in combining the ideas of aviation and cleaning into a meaningful whole. Likewise the arrangement of a carton under a dining-room chair, with a kitchen wastebasket beside it, is difficult to reconcile with usual notions about dining rooms. Arrangement of objects according to principles of practicality, accessibility, and usage offers other ways of integrating details into a whole.

The codification of ideas in material terms, in regard to both small objects and more sizable constructions, is largely related to notions of order. But, unlike the order dictated by logic, **the order of objects** depends largely upon physical reality. The laws of physics determine the construction of an object. The material determines its appearance and usage. Human needs dictate an object's function and shape. Agreements between people govern the manner of arrangement of several objects, and during any historical period these styles were known to most people within a particular cultural group. Thus there was possible a shared understanding of the use and interpretation of object language. However, above and beyond all this, and in a way similar to pictorial representation, objects can become a kind of international language. In the last analysis, practical objects are relatively free of the limitations imposed by class, caste, and race; instead they are controlled by considerations of a more universal nature: the ability to serve men at a given time for a given purpose.

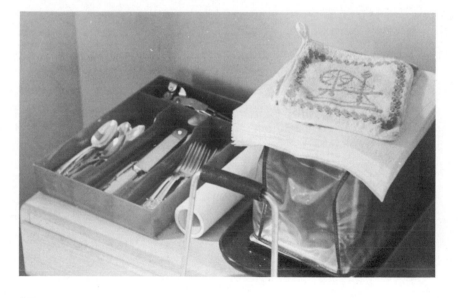

35

OBJECT ARRANGEMENT FOR PURPOSE OF ACTION

10. OBJECT, WORD, AND NUMBER

Letters of the alphabet may be combined into words that, when perceived by human beings, may evoke associations bearing upon their past experiences. Words can be replaced by objects whose material, surface structure, style, size, and shape are equally capable of evoking memories. Thus any letter, word, or material article may take on symbolic properties. However, the principal difference between word and object is that **words** in their very nature **are necessarily symbolic and referential**, and **objects may or may not be**. Lapel buttons, medals and decorations, sports trophies, statues, and objects of art are obviously symbolic. In contrast, machinery and tools are primarily regarded as practical rather than symbolic, even though all practical articles may at times assume symbolic functions.

In contrast to words, some objects are used as **extensions** of our sense organs—binoculars and microscopes, for example, increase the scope of vision. Such objects as steamshovels and derricks not only extend the usefulness of our muscles but actually replace them. Perhaps the most significant difference between objects and words is the capacity of some objects to undergo energy transformations, to move, and in some cases to bring about pain and destruction. Poisons, drugs, electric currents, explosives, and radioactive substances are some of the more spectacular examples. Words, per se, never present quite this kind of danger; the informative aspects of words must be implemented by action in order to be physically felt.

Consequently, objects exert upon the human being an influence vastly different from that of words. Spoken words are essentially perceived as sound signals, printed words as visual signals. Objects, through their material body, surface texture, weight, and often their aroma, taste, and temperature, also **appeal to** our **proximity receivers**, conveying impressions that words are incapable of producing. Therefore, words are perceived by one or two sensory modalities, objects usually by more. Furthermore, when objects are steadily observed, they exert a continual influence upon our sense organs without necessarily producing perceptive fatigue; human tolerance for the repetition of the same word has its limitations. Paintings and other objects of art are frequently studied for hours on end, and people may look at objects in their homes, in museums, and in store windows repeatedly and for extended periods of time without necessarily feeling boredom or a sense of redundancy. Therefore, in object language, the immediacy of the object is continuously emphasized. Its effect is persuasive and stringent; its appeal is not only to spectatorship but to action as well; and its implications suggest usage.

The object as symbol

The object as practical
article

The practical object as sidewalk
symbol

WORD AND OBJECT

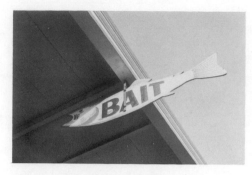

Word and symbolic object in
mutual complementation

Words alone: the object as
frame

The whole story: a nonverbal
comment through format

Word, price, and object in mutual reinforcement

We mean business

Get it while it lasts

Standard bill of fare

Raised lettering for swank

We greet your defect with seriousness and responsibility

So much for the analogy between word and object. Matters become more complicated when word sequences and conglomerations of objects are considered. In linguistics, the field of **syntactics** is given over to the study of the mutual relationship of verbal signs to each other. A corresponding relationship in object language (106) is expressed through the combination of materials, surface structure, color, and shape to produce an object that embodies the functions of noun, adjective, verb, and adverb all in one. Finally, the sequences of sentences leading to the expression of an idea are achieved in object language through the arrangement of several articles in space; the idea that is then expressed may be called a **theme**.

Written speech is broken up by the period, the comma, the colon, the semicolon, the question mark, and the exclamation point. Along with these punctuation marks, the arrangement of printed words into sentences, paragraphs, and chapters constitutes nonverbalized comments and instructions to the reader about how ideas and thoughts are intended to be broken up. Correspondingly in spoken language, slowing down the rate of speech at the end of a sentence, pausing, and speaking louder and softer are the verbal and gestural equivalents of punctuation marks. In object language, similar devices make for emphasis. Objects may be grouped in such a way that the eye perceives imaginary boundary lines that are designed to break up space, inasmuch as two clusters of articles in otherwise empty space are usually treated as separate entities.

The entity of the written word is determined by material features; when words and letters are printed, written, painted, or drawn, they necessarily have a material body—often quite a substantial one. The **material aspects of letters** may indicate subtleties that the literal meaning of the word is quite incapable of expressing. The reader of a book is influenced and guided, not only by print on paper, but also by the style of the typography, the quality of the paper, the margins, and other features of book format. We tend to be consciously aware of the signifying functions of letters and words, but remain far less aware of the nonverbal modifiers contained in material, color, and shape. When objects are added to illustrate words, or when words are used to amplify statements coded in terms of objects, such additions may modify either word or object to such an extent that the meaning of the combined whole differs radically from that of its component parts. For example, large bronze numerals, precisely mounted on a polished oak door, convey a sense of solidity and dignity and offer hints to the visitor as to how those who live behind such a door would like to be met. If the same numbers were painted by hand with red enamel on an aluminum door, the impression would be different.

The mutual complementation of object and word appears with particular prominence in shop windows and on the streets. Each verbal statement is usually held together by a **frame** or other device that has been placed in the visual environment of motorists and pedestrians to influence their actions (59). Printed words may appear alone or in combination with objects; when the objects are for sale, they may indicate prices, names, or labels. Occasionally words may spread across a store front and tell practically a whole story.

Another way of altering the impression of printed words is achieved through the **style of lettering** and the spacing of print. Through typographical characteristics of signs and announcements in and around stores, shopkeepers not only express their own personalities but also set the tone that governs relationships with the customer. A careful observer of such

ANNOUNCING SANITARY FACILITIES

signs is tuned in advance to the type of reception he may expect. In the orthopedic store window, for example, type font and vellum-shaped shield suggest the sort of prestige conferred by a diploma, conveying the idea that the customer is in reliable hands. The whitewashed bologna sign, combined with the toilet-paper announcement, screams for the customer's attention. "Do Not Enter" in heavy black letters expresses a stern command that might be interpreted as an invitation to trespass if a more delicate lettering had been used. The luxury store, through its raised letters on a soft rug, evenly spaced, and interwoven with art objects, conveys a feeling of solitude and sophistication; the lighted menu of the chain restaurant, through its lettering, primes the customer to expect a rather run-of-the-mill cuisine.

One of the most versatile ways of indicating variations in the meaning of one word is found in the announcement of **sanitary facilities**. Through words or signs, people are guided to plumbing. In some localities, use of such facilities by both sexes is permitted. The verbal designation of such nonexclusive stations is manifold: "bathroom," "washroom," "lavatory," "toilet," "comfort station," "W. C.," "john," "head," "can," "biffy," "privy."

In other localities, especially in public places, men and women are provided with separate sanitary facilities. Here, amplifying statements abound, indicating not only the social characteristics of the clientele, but referring even to such matters as the kind of humor that is considered fitting. Accordingly, the colloquial designations of these stations rarely coincide with their written counterparts, and some of these expressions are more commonly seen than heard. The selection of a particular noun—such as "Men," "Gentlemen," or "Gents"—not only makes a statement about the status of the male that may be expected to use the facilities, but also expresses the mandatory nature of the announcement. The sign as a whole may hold out a promise of comfort, invitation, or restriction, or it may prohibit particular activities, as in the beach resort's admonition against using their "gentlemen's" room for dressing or undressing. Styles of lettering and the format of signs still further amplify the messages expressed in the printed word. In rustic settings, for example, announcements are not infrequently accompanied by arrows that point vaguely and blend into the landscape to such a degree as to be of little help in an emergency. In contrast, the filling-station "rest rooms" of the large oil companies are usually announced in huge letters that are easily visible to the motorist. A solicitude about "registration," "cleanliness," and "inspection" is conveyed not only in words; a sense of dignity in keeping with the seriousness of the need is sometimes added through heraldic format, recalling the "diploma" in Plate 38.

The **language of abbreviation** is particularly useful for the benefit of the motorist, to those in a hurry, and a necessity for children, foreigners, and illiterates. One of the most efficient ways of making a brief and succinct statement is to combine simple words with pictures or objects. Thus great specificity, exemplification, and repetition can be achieved without a sense of the cumbersome. Simplicity of effect is often dependent upon complex word-sign-object language—for example, the large black arrow covering the entire wall of a liquor store. This pointer stabs toward the corner and guides the customers to the entrance. It aims at arousing curiosity and, through its immense size, sounds an urgent, demanding, and insistent note. Since the arrow is black painted on white, it does double duty by standing for the name of the store.

Statements in commercial, private, or public life can be phrased in terms that may be exclusive or inclusive, shorthand or longhand, repeated or nonrepeated, illustrated or non-

40

A BRIEF AND CONCISE STATEMENT

HOW TO BE BRIEF

Illustration

Pinpointing

Identification

Exemplification (outside a junkyard)

Translation

Embodiment and redundancy

illustrated, verbal or nonverbal. Sometimes it is expedient to **translate** a word or two into a symbol, because the visual effect may be so characteristic as to obviate verbal explanation. Similar to pidgin English and to other languages of culture contact, a mixture of words and things for purposes of communication denotes the fluid boundaries between the universe of words and the universe of objects. That they can be used in alternate ways clearly demonstrates the communicative value of material articles. The stylized hand, reaching out in welcome, symbolizes the name of a restaurant: "The Glad Hand." At other times, the device of illustrating comes into play, as on the canopy of a bowling alley. The pin and balls define the sporting nature of the estabishment, and the kegler is thus provided with a sample of what to expect inside without having to decipher verbal inscriptions. In front of a fenced-in junk yard, weatherbeaten dummies and a washing machine exemplify the kind of merchandise that is for sale. John's Lighthouse Grill repeats its verbal statement by embodiment in a three-dimensional structure.

Abbreviated statements are based on a number of assumptions: first, that the abbreviations used are supposedly intelligible to those who will see them; second, that the brevity does not omit relevant information; and third, that the symbols chosen evoke the desired associations. For example, the barber shop, with an almost classic simplicity, assumes that the passer-by is familiar not only with the condensed and flattened version of the barber's symbol, but also with the owner's prices, personnel, and facilities, which are not visible from the outside.

The language of abbreviation also comes into play in **"unmentionable" topics.** Trusses, braces, corsets, and girdles are exhibited in show windows because men or women who suffer from imperfections are frequently embarrassed about asking for such objects in verbal terms. To see these items exhibited offers hope that their problems will be met with understanding and skill. Inducements to conceal or banish ill health are rather successful in a civilization where youth and strength are at a premium. To arouse or meet the concern of the public with appearance, the subtle appeal to fear and dejection along with the invocation of the consequences of not caring for the body are conjured in the spectator by the grimness of some of these displays. Before studying such windows, the passer-by may cast an embarrassed look around, as if he were doing a wrong thing or perhaps acknowledging a personal imperfection.

Object language lends itself ideally for making statements about **value**. To make two things of different structure and function comparable, certain qualities of both must first be abstracted. Lacking other identifying information, we may speak, for example, of a $25,000-a-year executive or a $30-a-week soda jerk. In the world of trade, value and price are emphasized; in most stores, price tags label most objects. This mixed verbal-object language enables the customer to compare teapots with teapots or teapots with shirts. The way in which prices are announced may contain additional and subtle comments about the value of an object. Large price tags usually indicate that the wares are inexpensive; small price tags may indicate that the object is expensive, or they may suggest that price, within a given bracket, falls into the customary range. Shoppers can be expected to know the prevailing prices of food items and other daily necessities. Deviations from generally established values are then indicated by signs advertising specials, bargains, and sales. Some stores dispense altogether with the announcement of prices, anticipating that their customers are

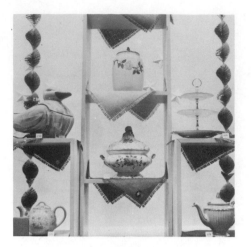

Large objects and small price
tags indicate regular price

Out-of-line prices are specially announced

Many items with no price tag
indicate reasonable value

A single item with no price tag
indicates expensive wares

Objects with large price tags
indicate cheapness

acquainted with the usual value range for a given type of merchandise. Arrangement, then, with a certain sense of delicacy, does indicate the relative position in that particular scale of valuation. Multiple objects indicate that the items are sold at the lower end of that particular range. The display of single objects indicates that the value is likely to be at the upper end of the scale, forewarning the prospective buyer of a stiff price indeed.

11. THE LANGUAGE OF IDENTIFICATION AND RECOGNITION

No programmatic analysis has ever done justice to what may be called the **atmosphere** of a house, a block, or a section of a city. The flavor of a particular part of town, for example, depends not only upon architectural style and the nature of whatever domestic or commercial activity may take place there, but upon the way every aspect of the material environment is interwoven with patterns of living. This combination of factors, with their esthetic, emotional, and intellectual connotations, may set expectations of what may be encountered. Unescorted society matrons are not usually found in the tougher waterfront areas. A cowboy on vacation is not likely to seek entertaiment in the most refined neighborhoods of a large city. When a person identifies a particular atmosphere, it helps him to anticipate what kind of people he may confront, what kind of language is likely to be spoken, and even what kind of action may take place. Indeed, the divisions of a city into residential, commercial, and industrial sections are embodied in zoning laws that have come about as a result of human activities.

Objects fulfill a highly **symbolic function** when people use them to announce what they are and what they do. Especially in a democracy, where people are—ideally speaking—supposed to be equals, objects have the useful function of announcing inequalities that, for reasons of taste and conformity, cannot be expressed in words. Additionally, there are things that cannot be said about others without the risk of slander, as well as things a person does not say about himself without seeming conceited, anxious for compliments, or arrogantly humble. These hazards may be circumvented by the use of object language, which can operate twenty-four hours a day, is accessible to both rich and poor, literate and illiterate, and may be visible at a considerable distance. Individuals may thus announce their membership in particular groups by wearing club insignia in the form of lapel buttons, rings, or watch-chain keys.

Interwoven with such officially stated memberships are those of a more informal nature. Foremost among these are the groupings according to sex, caste, class, status, nationality, and religion. The concept of social class, for example, bears upon the fact that vertical stratification exists in most societies. **Status**, therefore, refers to an attribute that is determined by asking the question: "Who looks up to whom, and who looks down upon whom?" Statements about status are made implicitly, through the exhibition of skill, through display of property, and through selective association with people who have similar prestige; statements of social class are implicit in the neighborhoods in which people live, shop, drink, eat, and play. Skid road, with its rooming houses, missions, and pawnshops, houses a unique

Commercial atmosphere

Industrial atmosphere

Tourist atmosphere

44

THE STATUS OF DISTRICTS SPEAKS FOR ITSELF

American Christmas à la
Chinese

Santa Claus visits Little Italy

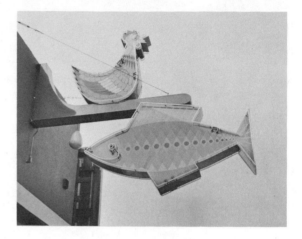

ANNOUNCEMENTS OF IDENTITY

Personal identification in a
suburban maritime setting

Identification by terseness
rather than by name

Identification through characteristics of
façade: an entrance to an entrance

The personal touch

Identification through unusual
architectural design

class—exclusive as well as excluded—whereas new suburban developments are ready to absorb all who are willing to conform to the prevailing standards and to pay for this privilege.

Most groups, however, do not live in isolation from each other, and where they intermingle the phenomenon of **culture contact** occurs. In the wider sense of the word, this involves not only change from one class to another but from foreign to native values and from civilian to military standards. Most of the persons who are geographically, socially, or culturally mobile meet with others who, like themselves, also attempt change of group membership. In America, minority groups bring with them their old ways of communicating and value systems as well as a growing readiness to change these for new ones. Thus when people move from Europe or Asia to America, they adapt, in due course of time, to the values and practices prevalent here. In this process of acculturation, some frequently retain their original characteristics for a long time; with others, the features of the old and the new cultures are closely intermingled without being completely fused. In the Italian and Chinese sections of larger cities, these changes are expressed not only verbally but nonverbally as well. For example, the lantern decoration in San Francisco's Chinatown during the holiday season combines Chinese style with American Christmas tradition: the little Chinese boy, in Oriental garb, has angel wings and sings "Noel." Santa Claus, a somewhat unfamiliar figure in the Mediterranean, decorates a facsimile fireplace in a restaurant-supply store window; his ruddy, Anglo-Saxon face, as well as the "Season's Greetings," almost overpowers the "old country" flavor of Italian coffee machines, double-necked bottles, and ravioli molds.

Persons are identified not only by their membership in social and cultural groups; they also identify themselves through **trade symbols**, which usually embody, in a condensed form, statements about their activities as tradesmen, craftsmen, or professionals. The barber pole, today a symbol of shaving and haircutting, goes back to the barber's original activity as a surgeon, the stripes symbolizing bandages and blood. The R is a symbol for "recipe"— "take thou"; combined with the mortar and pestle, it is a traditional mark of the pharmacist. In spite of the fact that many people have forgotten the origin of these two symbols, they are in widespread usage today. There are also more individualized object symbols, such as the hen, egg, and fish, which are of more recent origin.

Similarly, some uniforms, lapel buttons, hat insignia, and arm bands serve the purpose of identifying the wearer not so much as an individual but as a member of an occupational group. Occupational identity and role permit persons to find each other and to engage in commercial transactions. Thus the traffic cop, the judge, the physician, the train conductor, or the stewardess may be quickly identified vocationally. Such external identification greatly facilitates short-term communication—for example, when asking directions or when buying a ticket. The professional uniform is the personal counterpart of the trade symbol that denotes a particular business establishment.

Intermingled with symbols denoting occupation, public office, official role, or group membership are the marks that identify **unique individual features**. As trade symbols identify a place of work, and community insignia a public building, so may an individual characterize his residence in a particular way. This is noticeable in doorways and entrances —places where people are accustomed to look for just such identifying marks. However, the first over-all impression of a house may be radically modified after a closer look at house numbers, name plates, mailboxes, and doorbells, which together form a theme that may

Nihilism

Thoreau and "back to nature"

Hedonism

Existentialism

Theism

The philosophy of the common man

Painting

Chalking

Mixed media

Alteration

Engraving

differentiate the house from neighboring ones. Even though words may be used on mailboxes or under doorbells, the choice of lettering and their spacing supply a nonverbal and highly individual flavor. A specialty store, for example, located in a small, narrow street, announces itself by stunning and unusual architecture, the absence of any display of products, and an all but invisible name. The announcement is "effective" because it is generally known locally that the building is the work of Frank Lloyd Wright, a distinction not many stores can boast of; it arrests the attention even of those unaware of the identity of its designer. The hand-lettered sign, "We Clean Fish," placed below a decorative star suggests to the visitor the romantic notion of a wharf inhabited by fishermen, gourmets, and artists. On the other hand, commentary is pared down to the bone on the side of a house where a simple white line serves to outline the existence of an office.

Statements of identification may be routine, ostentatious, or bleak; they may indicate the economic success of the owner or say something about his tastes, hobbies, and social accessibility, and perhaps about his attitudes toward his neighbors and class. These statements often convey, moreover, something that a person thinks can bear repeating: that he is pleased by the look of his own name; that he finds the city preferable to the country; or that he believes life can be stripped to bare essentials.

Identification involves not only names, labels, and actions but also **attitudes and beliefs**. These are expressed in the preferences people show for certain ways of perceiving, thinking, expressing, or acting, or to certain theories of causality, determinism, and interrelationship. In short, beliefs are ways of dealing with information and with missing information. Even basic beliefs turn up repeatedly and strikingly in nonverbal statements that seem to sum up recognized ways of life. A gigantic metal frankfurter, a woebegone entranceway, and a mutilated recruiting poster emerge as declarations of various ways of regarding the world. These declarations are almost as intelligible as though those responsible had chalked their philosophies of life on signs and walls and windows, like the passer-by who expresses his moods and his views about the world on houses, stairways, toilets, elevators, sidewalks, posters, and subways. Most of these artists carry with them the tools of their trade—chalk, paint, pencils, soap, or knives. The **passer-by as decorator** is usually an adolescent, a "revolutionary," or a person who abhors plain surfaces; his comments traditionally pertain to social criticism, politics, or gossip. Places where property rights are in abeyance or where young people are apt to loiter—street corners and bus stops—are favorite working places for those specializing in spontaneous and random doodling. The commentaries written or drawn along the paths of human traffic correspond to whispering campaigns. These messages to the world at large are a form of expression engaged in by those who otherwise are rarely heard.

12. APPEAL AND SOCIAL CONTROL THROUGH MATERIAL THINGS

Verbal commands, suggestions, and hints are common ways of influencing people in a direct manner. However, the resistance to such approaches increases with insistence and repetition —drawbacks that are less likely to present themselves when indirect and nonverbal methods of influence are employed. Such methods involve three principal lines of approach: the first involves exhibiting objects with an implicit appeal to perception; the second involves the arrangement of articles in such a way that they can be used or tried out, where the appeal is essentially kinesthetic and muscular; and the third involves control of the traffic lanes on the highways, sidewalks, and interiors of stores or houses. All three methods involve control of social situations by using the predictable needs of human beings for specific ends or by arranging physical facilities in the hope that people will not bother to change them. Who shall meet whom, when, where, and perhaps for how long can thus be determined in advance.

Appeal to Perception

Stores and places of entertainment not only must identify themselves so that the customers can come to see them; in turn they must, if they wish to survive, **appeal selectively** to customers who need their goods and services. The specialty store in particular has the task of attracting customers whose needs and interests may result in a business transaction.

An initial distinction among potential customers lies in differentiating men and women, the old and the young, workmen and luxury trade. Women, for example, are not likely to be interested in engines; indeed, most women consider an engine or a boat more of a competitor than an object of curiosity. Exhibitions of hardware or motor parts will not usually stop a woman passing on the street. Men, in contrast, rarely look at window displays of "foundation garments," except surreptitiously. Jewelers and other luxury stores make a particular appeal to persons currently interested in a member of the opposite sex.

The cues that serve as recognition signals for a **particular clientele** are of considerable subtlety, and are often implicit in the arrangement of display as a whole. The mural in front of Dougherty's bar has as its subject matter a woodland lake scene. It not only covers the entire front, making its point about privacy, but also, in one of its details—the meeting of the elks—has something to say about isolation as a problem of lonely people in a big city. The permanence of the mural gets over the idea that it is an anchorage for neighborhood regulars. In contrast, the South Pacific island atmosphere offered by a fashionable restaurant beckons both the Pacific traveler and the sentimentalist; the artists' bar extends an invitation

CUES FOR PARTICULAR CLIENTELES

For Bohemians

For gourmets and seekers of atmosphere

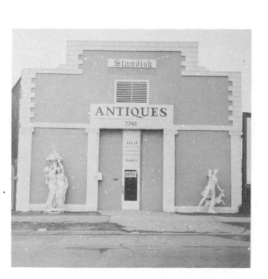

For connoisseurs

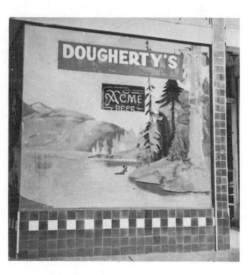

For neighborhood regulars

Romance of the humdrum

Dream girl as added attraction

The home-cooked touch

Nothing left for fantasy with
a naturalistic model

Invitation for fantasy elaboration
when only parts are shown

Real involvement with a two-
dimensional presentation

to those who want to throw off the yoke of conformity and rub elbows with actual or would-be Bohemians; the shopper for antiques is alerted by the elegant formality of the lettering, the symmetry of the building, and the classic art motif.

The problem of facilitating the meeting of buyers and sellers is met only through cues of mutual identification, since some people tend to react more to the **line of approach**— the "how" of action—than to marks of identity—the "what" of action. The line of approach is expressed sometimes with greater urgency in the intimations of doorways, which set the expectations of those who enter. To promise, disappoint, intimidate, guide, or restrict people in their thoughts and actions is an art in itself; the efficient interpretation of such statements frequently lies in going far beyond their literal meaning. In addition, to overcome the feelings of anxiety, indecision, and reserve that frequently arise when people are asked to commit themselves before they are familiar with a situation, many establishments extend special invitations through conspicuously displayed signs and notices. A commercial establishment may express its special concerns by assuming a specific line of approach defining the social techniques and forms of relatedness. What is suggested here is not exclusiveness of identity but conformity in terms of action.

The whitewash lettering announces the changing variety of merchandise in the second-hand store. The unobstructed view into the store invites rummaging for "finds" inside. The verbal announcement of Mary's hamburgers indicates, through the presence of the flowers and the handwritten sign, that atmosphere as well as food goes into the making of a restaurant, and that this one is homelike, personal, and improvised. The airline's display takes the line that the destination advertised is one of lush foliage where a hula girl eagerly awaits the passenger.

Various **dimensions** may be used to evoke fantasies and bodily sensations. Three-dimensional dummies, clothed or unclothed, do not seem to convey sensations of warmth or sensuality. To produce such effects, decorators usually fall back on photographs or paintings. However, the idea of sensuality can sometimes be relayed to the spectator by the isolation of parts of the body or clothing, leaving it to the individual's capacity for fantasy to fit bodies into clothing and to complete what is left unexpressed. Apparently a two-dimensional reproduction or a three-dimensional facsimile in close-up perspective is more effective for such purposes than an elaborate naturalistic model that acts as a hindrance to fantasy.

Summons for Action

The placement of a certain kind of object in a strategic location may at times substitute for any explanations and instructions. The effect is achieved only with objects that can be presupposed to be familiar and whose usage is known. Then the instruction carried by the object points to either doing or not doing. Strategically placed barbed wire, for example, transmits a warning to stay away. The box placed strategically on top of a pile of newspapers on a sidewalk appeals to the honesty of the passer-by, and presupposes that he knows the current price of the newspapers and will deposit the correct amount in the slot. Lowered metal flags on the sides of the rural mailboxes indicate that no mail has been placed in the box, and therefore carry a definite instruction to action, here limited to transactions between the postman and the particular boxholder.

Commands, instructions, and warnings transmitted through object language are offi-

WHAT SHAPES OF SIGNS CAN CONVEY

OCTAGONAL
Command to stop

CIRCULAR
Warning of railroad crossing

SHIELD
U. S. Highway

OBLONG RECTANGLE
Directions about local regulations

DIAGONAL SQUARE
Suggestion to slow down

SQUARE
Directions on what's ahead

INSTRUCTION AND COMMAND

Stay out

Deposit; or pick up

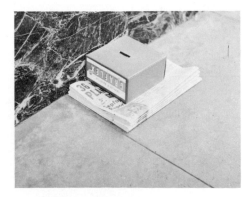

Pay and help yourself

USAGE AND SUGGESTION

Take it away

Watch your fenders

Use whatever applies

cially used in directing the motorist. The shape of **highway signs** indicates the verbal sub-ject matter of the sign. The motorist who has little time for reading is thus primed, through format, for the kind of information he will get on a sign of a particular shape.

In a technical civilization like ours, order and tidiness are considered to be of prime im-portance. Few if any **traces of living** escape the mop and the vacuum cleaner; even streets are washed. When so many traces of living are taken away, often people lack the necessary cues of what has taken place and what they may do. Unless such traces are replaced by some kind of verbal instructions, another kind of disorder is likely to result. But individuals differ in their eagerness to obliterate traces of living, and those traces that are allowed to stay may contain statements about pride and sentimentality as well as indifference and ex-pediency. A garbage can piled high with debris, placed on a sidewalk, is an unmistakable suggestion to the collection men. A scraped wall surface with large patches of missing plas-ter and paint warns the motorist of cramped quarters. Door knocker, lock, doorknob, and mailbox invite a person to announce his presence, enter, or leave a message.

Objects can control movements of the body. In appraising the suitability of an object for personal use, an observer usually combines his perceptual impression of the object with considerations of his body image. He projects himself in action and, subsequently in an actual test, compares his achievement with his expectations. Often the actual test is con-sidered unnecessary, with the visual appraisal sufficing. The reader who smokes is invited to imagine himself seated in any of the easy chairs in Plate 56. How would it feel to flick ashes into the trays, or to reach for the matches? A strikingly complicated statement is con-veyed by the "contour" chair, whose tortured shape belies the bodily ease for which it is said to have been designed.

Practical objects of daily use tend to be placed in an accessible manner. Some people, however, set up obstacle courses for themselves and others. The varieties of such obstruc-tions can be numerous and even ingenious. For example, on the kitchen counter, pill boxes, pot holders, and pudding packages sit on top of each cannister, and the only uncovered container is obstructed in front. The esthetic "ensemble" in the living room consists of books artfully blocked by decorative objects. The compromises thus made between practicality and comfort, on the one hand, and well-being and effort, on the other, shape the interaction between people and between people and objects.

Design for Meeting

The life of domestic animals is, among other things, controlled through the erection of fences, flap doors, or the placement of food and water in particular locations. Although the control of human situations is implemented through verbal and nonverbal actions, manipulation of bar-riers, openings, and other physical arrangements is rather helpful. Meeting places can be appropriately rigged so as to regulate human traffic and, to a certain extent, the network of communication. An auditorium in which chairs are placed in parallel rows, where people cannot face each other, is unlikely to provoke much discussion; an amphitheater, on the contrary, makes a lively discussion more probable, because people are able to see each other.

Even particular kinds of human interaction are frequently steered, facilitated, or modified by the **physical nature of establishments**, which may indicate where possible meetings

THE KINESTHETICS OF USAGE

How do you reach the ashtray while seated?

Decorative barricade

Covered covers

You can't tell until you've tried it

may occur—in a car, on a sidewalk, or in a store. Announcements of special meeting places for the transaction of particular tasks are recognizable through their strategic location and special format—in lettering, shape, and color. Although the content of the statements may be expressed in words, recognition from a distance is based upon nonverbal cues. The post office announces, through a particular type of hood, the existence of a mailbox specifically designed for the motorist. Since this is an innovation, the government feels the necessity of pointing out its use in verbal terms as well. The fire department, in keeping with the emergency nature of its function, is more succinct. The point is implied that any person, after breaking the glass and pushing the button, will meet the representatives of the fire department at this spot a few minutes later. The very architecture of the drive-in is designed to allow the customer to enjoy the customary surroundings of his car without the effort of getting out or dressing for the occasion. However, if the customer is of a more gregarious and enterprising nature, he is still free to park his car and eat inside.

Meeting places are not confined to outdoors. The interiors of both stores and houses are honeycombed with potential sites for interpersonal activities. Physical arrangements elicit expectations; they may instruct to some degree: "This, and not that"; "Here, not there." Most stores make sure that their customers are immediately confronted by merchandise. By being forced to walk between displays of merchandise, the customers are informed of what is available. Care is taken to place chairs and tables for comfort at strategic locations, and in full view of the merchandise, with a salesman or salesgirl in readiness to take the order.

In private homes, arrangements of **furniture** and accessory objects likewise designate and control the "where" and "how" of interaction. Such factors as the nature of the lighting, the placing of tables, and the grouping of chairs and couches may further modify interpersonal exchanges. Chairs faced obliquely attenuate direct confrontation. A table between two chairs sets up a sort of barrier. This obstacle, however, may reassure the participants that excessive closeness will not be forced upon them, and with this reassurance they may achieve more intimate communication than would otherwise be possible. Shape and arrangement of furniture provide clues about how easily and conveniently the furniture may be approached and what degree of comfort may be anticipated. The two dining-room arrangements offer very different statements about comfort: the hard wicker chairs welcome; the "soft" dining chairs pushed up to the table are less cordial.

The subdivision of a house into separate rooms creates physical and psychological barriers that force the residents to stake out **private corners** for themselves. The usual bachelor quarters are in themselves one big private corner, but in a family dwelling these special places are reduced to diminutive size. The lady's dressing table, for example, is organized around principles that are not challenged by the other members of the household, and hence stakes its claim as a place of refuge. The private corner contains a statement of sufferance as well as of resistance: would the boxer be allowed his special place on the couch if he were not decorative? A unique phenomenon—a sort of communal private corner—is the little straw basket dish, about which one of the owners explained: "That is where we empty our pockets."

FURNITURE AND INTERACTION CONTROL

Tête-à-tête at right angles

Make yourself at home

Sit down by invitation only

Interpersonal hurdle

CONTACT BY REMOTE CONTROL

Scheduled

Emergency

FACE-TO-FACE CONTACT

You come to us

We come to you

Splendor of privacy

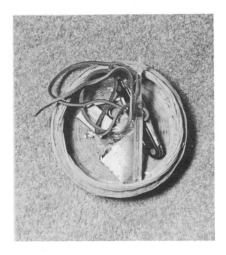

Communal privacy

Privacy may depend upon tolerance

13. THE ORGANIZATION OF THE MATERIAL ENVIRONMENT AS PERSONAL EXPRESSION

Foremost in the array of things that men have ordered are the objects with which they surround themselves in their own homes. Since houses are primarily places to live in, this fact influences the distribution of space, the installation of accessories, the kind of ventilation and lighting, along with other such practical considerations. In addition, and to varying degrees, the architectural trends of a particular period may be incorporated in the structure and decoration of the building. Such factors as geography, climate, and the availability of certain construction materials play an influential part. Earlier generations in America built in the colonial, New England, or Spanish adobe styles, among others. Just now, particularly in the far West, where construction is a flourishing industry, the dominant style is a stereotyped "modern," usually featuring redwood and other natural wood walls, goldfish bowl windows, patios, and grapestake fences.

Most **styles** evolve gradually and develop as a body of knowledge is accumulated about particular ways of living. When habits change and technical innovations are introduced, established styles may be modified to the extent of becoming hybrid or chaotic. At present, certain stylistic stereotypes are widespread in housing projects and suburban developments. It is largely the well-to-do who have the chance to escape architectural uniformity and regimentation and to have houses built which suit their individual needs, provided they are not, like the *nouveaux riches*, concerned with converting buildings and grounds into statements of wealth and power. More individualistic is the dwelling of the home craftsman, which is likely to be filled with gadgets "to make life simple"; the home of the artist—half living quarters and half workshop—bears the imprint of altogether different values.

Not everyone is fortunate enough to live in a structure built to meet the demands of his own taste. Consequently, not all houses express their occupants' individuality. Few who live in rented places, for example, can afford to remodel or redecorate. Even so, every building indicates in some way whether or not it is representative of those who live in it. This is particularly true about interiors, where the nature and arrangements of possessions say a great deal about their owners views of existence. In contrast, the aims of merchants are usually more sharply defined than those of home owners; businessmen are mainly out to sell; but people in their private lives have intentions that may be far more complex and diversified.

In the interpretation of houses, a question frequently arises that bears upon the **purposes and intentions of the owners**: are the things they display directed toward others, or are they for home consumption, or both? Sometimes this question gets a direct answer; there are those

EXAMPLES OF ATMOSPHERE IN THREE DIFFERENT HOUSES

Spreading

Piling

Shelving

Dumping

frank enough to admit that their homes have been consciously built and furnished as show places—to impress others, to create the pretense of or actually to honor a family tradition, or to suggest a high credit rating or a large income. Others seem relatively indifferent to public opinion, and say that they decorate solely for their own pleasure; objects are largely valued for themselves alone, and rooms are arranged chiefly to serve the inhabitants of the house comfortably. In still another category are those home owners who endeavor to conform rigidly to neighborhood patterns. They are uninterested in originality and do not strive to outdo their neighbors, finding satisfaction in blending into the area as much as possible without attracting attention.

Every interior betrays the **nonverbal skills** of its inhabitants. The choice of materials, the distribution of space, the kind of objects that command attention or demand to be touched —as compared to those that intimidate or repel—have much to say about the preferred sensory modalities of their owners. Their sense of organization, the degree of freedom left to imagination, their coerciveness or esthetic rigidity, their sensitivity and fields of awareness —all are revealed in their houses. Child psychiatrists use play techniques to observe children expressing their foremost concerns through creative activities. Psychiatrists working with adults need only study the material environment with which individuals surround themselves to secure fresh insights into their relationships to objects, people, and ideas. The contrast between a meticulously kept mansion inhabited by an elderly couple and a small home filled with children, where marks of living are found everywhere, is one that needs no comment.

Ideas of Order

Through the doorway, into the hall, through the downstairs rooms, and up the stairs—this is the route of the visitor who is being "shown through" a house. At the end of the tour, and after viewing the rooms in succession, he is left with a sense of the prevailing **atmosphere.** The kinds of furniture, the arrangement of living space, the use of color—even to such details as bird cages or ashtrays—contribute toward the *Geist* created by its inhabitants, which is as characteristic of them as their names, their address, or their very fingerprints. Even when people move to a new house, the atmosphere that is based upon object arrangement and subdivision of space usually remains basically unchanged.

In the course of time, man accumulates a variety of things that threaten to clutter the home. He is faced with the problem of putting things together so that he may locate them when they are needed. The more objects accumulate, the more difficult is the maintenance of **order**, which in turn causes one person to leave a trail marked with debris and another to cover every trace. People have their preferred ways of storing: through piling, shelving, spreading, dumping, aligning, or through exposing or hiding. The storage of things need not, however, lead to stereotyping. Objects lend themselves to highly personal arrangement —even objects of everyday use. Thus the kinds of pots and pans, forks and ladles, and other kitchen utensils, and their placement around a stove, may perhaps indicate how the housewife feels about cooking. Similar considerations apply to the housing of such relatively uniform items as books. Since books may be used as reference works, tools of the trade, collector's items, for entertainment, or as a substitute for wallpaper, their arrangement may betray their owners as bookworms, casual readers, or merely decorators. Even toothbrushes and related toilet articles can be placed in a tasteful manner; as contemporary and ordinary an object as a telephone may take on period flavor when it has a doily underneath it.

Over and above considerations of economy of space, however, are the varying ideas of order that induce an individual to store bits of information, cataloguing or filing them so that they may be readily available when needed. Information is usually arranged in terms of subject matter, such as bread, horse, automobile, or eating, riding, driving. This type of arrangement depends upon "subject thinking" wherein the predicate is merely qualifying the subject. However, there are those who arrange information around the qualifying and relativistic terms of the predicate, such as high, fast, or green. In other words, things that are high or move quickly or have a green color are filed together. Extreme cases of **predicate thinking** characterize the condition known as schizophrenia (4). Through the orderly arrangement of objects, human beings obviously express their thinking. In object language, subject thinking shows up in the purposeful placement of things; predicate thinking, in meaningless placement. Such is often true when decoration for decoration's sake loses sight of formal, practical, and esthetic values, and when considerations of color, form, geometry, symmetry, and unrelated symbolism bear little relationship to ordinary problems of order. Sometimes decorators assume the role of the "pure artist"—one who is unsure of his audience, indifferent to it, or in the process of creating a "new" audience. He invades the territory of abstract symbolism where the signs—here the subject—are related to each other but are not necessarily signifying. This strategy may sometimes lead to creations that are stunning, fantastic, and original; just as often it leads to effects that are merely puzzling, involved, or obscure.

Decoration

Decoration involves embellishment and adornment. But in the language of objects, decoration is also a statement about the object that is decorated. Like the smile that may accompany a satirical remark, identifying it as a friendly gesture rather than as a hostile threat, decoration instructs the onlooker in various ways. It can inform a person whether a curtain is meant to shut out the light or whether it is thought of as a space-filling piece of drapery. Wallpaper can indicate the activities that are expected to take place in a room, and the one who chooses it can convey to visitors and family members alike instructions that they might be unwilling to accept if set forth in verbal terms.

Whereas one kind of decoration aims at an appeal to the personal, another kind attempts to achieve an impersonal effect. For example, the diversified ramifications of a large corporation, store, or public institution are difficult for people to conceptualize. How, then, can a firm with thousands of stockholders and numerous directors be figuratively represented to the man on the street? Some of the representatives of large corporations seem to feel that this end is achieved best by the adoption of a trademark, assuming that such a symbolic figure as a statue, a picture, or an animal removes the mask of anonymity and presents the organization and its services in a more appealing light. Since personification of a store or institution is rarely carried out in terms of the starkly naturalistic, it usually represents in some way an idealization that necessarily constitutes either a simplification or an embellishment. It often amounts to a nonverbal slogan.

DAILY ROUTINE AND PERSONAL TOUCH

The art of making a wall out of books

The dainty telephone

The implements of an enthusiast

The lonely volume

The esthetics of dental care

Emphasis on subject

Subject and predicate

Emphasis on predicate

THREE KINDS OF DISPLAY

Let the product speak for itself

Let the label show

Stun the onlooker

In contrast to the stores that keep their merchandise behind glass, some establishments put no barrier between the customer and the product. Such enterprises as hot-dog stands and ice-cream trucks thus convey the idea that their merchandise is supposedly fresh and that the middleman is omitted. Their wares are sometimes advertised by signs, but more often advertising is omitted altogether because the products speak for themselves.

Frequently the object itself dictates whatever decoration may be used. Its shape, size, consistency, and color determine the range of methods used in adorning it. Routine articles or objects that have neither a particularly distinguishing shape nor color are frequently rescued from obscurity by enclosures and **wrappings.** Many articles are boxed, wrapped, or packaged; considerations of identification, sanitation, advertising, and protection from the weather usually dictate this practice. Wrappings thus convey supplementary statements about the character of the merchandise—statements about perishability, value, and rarity. The wrapping of gifts is traditional—in part to produce the effect of surprise, in part to embellish and enlarge, and in part to titillate the recipient. Frequently the wrapping says more about the person responsible for it or for the one who carries the package than it does about what is inside. Wrappings can be further used to disguise or hide merchandise that a buyer might not care to be seen with.

Expression in wrapping ranges from partial to complete envelopment. Bakers who sell their products directly to the customer make a point of showing the bread as it has come from the oven in order to get the "homemade" point across. Crating or boxing is the usual protection for wares in transit, but the liquor dealer resorts to an unusual appeal; he displays the cases in which Rhine wine was shipped to enhance the idea of imported stock, and also to imply that people who buy such wine buy it by the case, or ought to. Ideas of envelopment as art for art's sake take a new turn in the case of the madonnalike bust in a luxury store. The figure is cosily and almost completely covered by articles of clothing and accessories—draped with a necktie, shrouded by a brocaded hood, and crowned, somewhat indecorously, with an elegant beaded evening bag.

In contrast, the display of an unadorned object may have the effect of arousing curiosity —especially in a culture where people are so continuously bombarded with supplementary and irrelevant messages. Display may highlight the object itself or its arrangement, background, shape, and color. Sometimes a single object is emphasized by isolation—placed strategically and prominently and separated from other distracting objects—or, as in the lobster stand, the arrangement of identical or very similar objects produces a unifying effect.

Where **pictures** are used in decorating, choices—modern or "old master," portrait or landscape, naturalistic or stylized—present themselves. Sometimes a selection is made to harmonize with the existing color scheme and furniture arrangement of a room. "I want four small green pictures to match the drapes in my living room and fit over the credenza." Others may be most concerned with subject matter: "I want a reproduction of water lilies for my bathroom." Still others concern themselves with matters of style or the name and reputation of the artist: "I want a Picasso." Some break the monotony of walls with pictures, or create a new monotony; others dispense with pictures altogether, and may use "view" windows instead. Some seem deeply concerned with the technique of hanging and mounting pictures, and others with their strategic placement and illumination. (See Plates 60, 66, 71, 73, 74).

BARE SURFACE AND SHIELD

HOUSE E: The Doily Theme

HOUSE F: Direct contact

HOUSE   F

HOUSE   E

Decoration also is a feature of urban existence. As asphalt, steel, and carbon monoxide close in on the city dweller, life may impress him as increasingly monotonous, nerve-racking, and precarious. When matters have reached this stage, the **"back to nature"** idea becomes more and more attractive. Then green plants, flowers, and fruit are introduced into apartments and homes, sometimes to the extent of converting living quarters into small-scale hothouses. Song birds and decorative botanical motifs are similarly called into service in an effort to satisfy unfulfilled longings for the world of springtime and renewal.

Personal Idiosyncracies

The most personalized form of expression in the world of objects is found in patterns of arrangement that are not exclusively intended as statements to others and are not solely dictated by the intrinsic characteristics of the objects themselves. To a larger extent these patterns seem to be statements of a person to himself. Some seem to be made with little or no real awareness that the choice and arrangement of objects are frequently made for the purpose of reminding oneself. For example, object arrangement in one house is marked by the naked **contact of object with surface**. The style of the other house features an interposed membrane between object and surface. This theme is developed to such an extent that even the chandelier is separated from the ceiling by a plaster rosette that assumes a position similar to that of the doily. The owners of House F apparently do not care whether the surfaces will be scratched by moving objects, and their security operations do not extend to the furniture. In House E, by contrast, protection is paramount, and is used so lavishly as to overwhelm both the surface and object and to become a purpose in itself.

Another type of idiosyncratic arrangement manifests itself in what might be called **vertical orientation**. Here, things not ordinarily arranged vertically are arranged on top of each other along a vertical coördinate. For example, most people who wear hats hang them on hat racks or put them away in closets when they take them off. The owners of House B make use of this method for ornamentation. The coat rack, with its cluster of precisely placed straw hats, is placed in the vicinity of other decorative straw articles, and becomes both utilitarian and decorative. That this resting place of headgear is more than coincidental is indicated by the picture of a carved wooden figure supporting a tray of coral in a hallway of this same house. A similar idiosyncracy is found in House E. The figure with the petaled wig stands on the newel post of the staircase. The china cowboy head with desert foliage emerging from his Stetson, also in this house, rests on a paper-towel container that does additional duty as a medicine shelf. These heads and crowns form a link in a series of vertical arrangements: the cowboy is topped by a wall lamp, the post is crowned by the girl's head, and the coat rack's verticality is emphasized by the vertical planking of the wall.

A particular vertical arrangement is evident in **altarlike assemblies** of objects. The dictionary defines an altar as "A raised structure, or any structure or place, on which sacrifices are offered or incense is burned in worship of a deity, ancestor, etc." In many homes, there are areas of central focus of interest framed by candles or other tall objects that suggest such a definition. Pictures of deities are usually replaced in contemporary houses by framed oil paintings or reproductions of a secular nature, but the presence of lamps and candles attests to the perhaps unconscious wishes of their owners to suggest an altar. Sometimes oil paintings are substituted by a mirror in which the self is given an opportunity to

HEADS AND CROWNS

HOUSE   E   HOUSE   B

OBJECTS ON PARADE

HOUSE   C

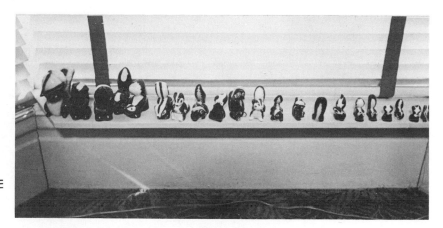

HOUSE   E

HOUSE   A

**THE IMPRINT
OF SHOWMANSHIP**

Wealth on parade

Studied casualness

Memento in a showcase

become the object of worship. Further bric-a-brac furnishes additional ornamentation of the kind found in holy places.

A **horizontal emphasis** is equally popular. Objects of similar size and shape are occasionally arranged so as to suggest soldiers at attention, lined up in single file. Arranged on shelves, on mantelpieces, or along the walls, such linear groupings emphasize the horizontal orientation of the owners. The flowerpots above the fireplace in House C are arranged in a trooplike fashion; the ceramic skunks on the windowsill of House E give a horizontal effect, not only by the alignment, but also by their size and shape. Finally, although the stools in House A could hardly have been arranged in any other way, they produce a horizontal effect that is reinforced by the scalloped lines of the candelabra.

Showmanship comes through most clearly in the placement of objects that may have considerable monetary value but little or no practical value. Objects displayed for the sake of showmanship demand to be looked at and often seem to be displayed to provoke comment. In contrast to other decorative articles that blend into the atmosphere of a room, such an object conveys its importance in the owner's eyes and the fact that he wishes to be acknowledged through acknowledgment of his object, or that he prides himself on being a collector or a connoisseur.

The imprint of showmanship is usually marked by effects that are intense, contrasting, unusual, and often contrary to expectations. These effects are achieved through the use of objects that impinge upon the onlooker's time and perceptual capacity so that he is able to identify the intention of the owner as one of competition in the field of exhibition. The fact that an article is impressive in itself does not imply that its owner's showmanship is outstanding. Within the framework of a social class or group culture, expert showmanship—in spite of its aggressiveness—is forgiven and tolerated; on the other hand, poor showmanship is more likely to irritate the onlooker and to provoke his scorn.

14. THE SYNTAX OF OBJECT LANGUAGE

Just as certain interior and window decorators, layout specialists, and installation directors of museums arrange objects in ways so individual as to make their signatures superfluous, so do the inhabitants of apartments and houses arrange objects in individually characteristic ways. People tend to express their preferences in taste through repetitive themes; for purposes of illustration, we have selected one theme from each of the six houses studied. It goes without saying that many themes—that is, systems of order and disorder—can be found in any dwelling. However, almost all interiors we had occasion to see, and certainly those that were photographed, seem to show some hierarchical order; some of these themes were ubiquitous and present in all rooms; others were more characteristic of either the master or mistress. Occasionally themes were an expression of a family style or climate of opinion. A number of our current styles of living make themselves felt through such patterns and themes, and are well recognized by others (141). They are embodied in such typifying words as "socialite," "Bohemian," or "bum." Few, however, are characterized by such clear-cut patterns. To an outsider a style may seem as random or chaotic as it may seem natural and ordered to an insider. Sometimes the style prevailing in a family has emerged in the course of existence without the participants being aware of the fact that they have agreed upon certain symbolization systems. The arrangement of objects then becomes an expression of the collective body. In the following pages, object arrangement has been documented to bring out the principles that weld object and décor into a whole. Placing object next to object, indeed, constitutes something of a syntax of object language. With the help of the index provided for each house, the reader may consult earlier plates for further illustration of the themes set apart in this section, in addition to the themes he may discover for himself.

LOOKING THROUGH: House A

This modern residence, on a hill overlooking the Pacific, displays a scorn of solid surfaces. Large windows and skylights are prominent features of the house; the rattan furniture and decorative objects are airy; the candelabra resembles fretwork; bottles and jars are transparent; mats and trays are reticulate.

In this atmosphere of openness, where the eye meets hardly any barriers, boundaries, although attenuated, are nevertheless distinctly delineated: there are curtains at the windows; the balcony balustrade is fashioned of thin strands of rope; the mat under the candelabra protects without concealing; the wall surfaces are unpainted, revealing the natural grain of the wood; a wire tray hangs on the wall but only partly hides it.

The emphasis upon openness and the apparent reluctance to conceal form the predominant theme of this house.

HOUSE A:

TO HIDE OR NOT TO HIDE, THAT IS THE QUESTION

Partitions needn't be walls, and
ceilings needn't be solid

Furniture and balustrade must
not obstruct the view

The grain and wood can still be
seen with a tray like this

Transparent storage

Protection without concealment

Additional pictures of House A are in the following plates: 32, Wood; 33, Conventional disorder; 36, The object as practical article; 56, How do you reach the ashtray while seated?; 62, The esthetics of dental care; 68, Objects on parade; 69, Studied casualness.

ORNAMENTATION OF FUNCTION: House B

Some houses resemble museums; others serve as camping grounds. House B shows a combination of both: from the long view of the living room to the detailed shot of the top of the kitchen stove, function and ornamentation are held in balanced interplay. In the living room: a Buddha views the scene from a vantage point on the bookshelves; a philodendron adorns the top of a storage cabinet; a decorative shawl is at hand to protect the sofa when the pet boxer makes it his bed (see Plate 59); green foliage graces the fireplace when it is not being used; cushions are piled in readiness for guests who wish to warm themselves by the fire. The same esthetic principles keep the bathroom from appearing plain and barren. The Oriental elephant not only breaks up the angular lines of the wooden staircase, but its head and back match the planes of individual steps. The shelf on the kitchen stove holds such essential items as timer, pepper grinder, and salt shaker; but the indispensable matches are in a decorative jar, introducing variety into an array of things that is usually highly stereotyped.

The theme of ornamentation of function thus expresses to others the owners' avocation of gathering objects of art around themselves and of placing them skillfully and knowingly among articles of daily usage. Ornamentation and utility go hand in hand, but rarely are they contained in one and the same object.

Additional pictures of House B are in the following plates: 35, Object arrangement for purpose of action; 36, The object as symbol; 56, Decorative barricade; 59, Privacy may depend upon tolerance; 62, The art of making a wall out of books, The implements of an enthusiast; 67, Heads and crowns.

HOUSE B:

USAGE AND BEAUTY

Stair theme repeated in the elephant

Decoration and practicality can live together

The owner's comment: "We don't mind lugging plants in and out of the fireplace"

Something to look at while drying the hands

Matches tastefully housed

HOUSE C: OCEANIC ORIENTATION

Beachcomber's harvest

The bridge

Detail of living-room floor: A boat
was built here

Combined living- and work-room

THE ROUGH HEWN DWELLING—HOUSE AS SHIP: House C

Highly polished floors; glittering table tops; gleam of silver, crystal, or ceramics; ruffles; draperies; soft cushions—none of these greets the visitor in House C. Instead, intricate carvings, rough finishes, and unpainted surfaces evoke an impression of ornateness and austerity combined to form the principal theme.

The house is treated as both a dwelling and a place of work. A loom stands in the living room; the floor is marked by traces of boat building; in another part of the living room a desk with a world globe, binoculars, ship's clock, and reference works on navigation bear witness to the occupation of the master of the house.

For centuries, plain surfaces and elaborate carvings were the mark of wooden sailing ships, where the presence of an ornate figurehead and a sumptuous captain's cabin contrasted with the stark planes of the deck and the crew's quarters. In keeping with nautical

Carving in captain's quarters

The kitchen's treasure chest

Plain comfort improvised

Crew's quarters

tradition, House C is characterized by straight lines and unadorned surfaces that exist side by side with elaborately carved bedsteads, cabinets, and chairs. This house—which literally faces the sea—reminds visitors and owners, through a collection of driftwood, shells, and other marine objects, that a vital and apparently all-absorbing interest governed it decoration. With scorn of plush and comfort and refutation of "contemporary style," the owners make an unequivocal statement about a highly individual philosophy of life.

Additional pictures of House C are in the following plates: 57, Make yourself at home; 59, Communal privacy; 60, Brick-and-stone fireplace; 61, Shelving; 68, Objects on parade.

THE LOGICAL PROGRESSION OF THEMES: House D

When sheer intellect governs the decoration of a house, an almost logical progression from one theme to another can be observed. House D is characterized by transitions that tie one decorative unit to the next one. The large philodendron in front of the living-room picture window blends the outdoors with the plant motif of the draperies. In the kitchen, hanging vines fulfill a similar function, binding the leaf patterns of the dinnerware with the wallpaper. Ivy growing through the bars of a birdcage is almost mirrored in the wallpaper serving its background. Further illustrations of this theme are the vertical arrangement of four still-life reproductions in which flowers and leaves figure prominently, and a wavy line, not unlike vine tendrils, which ties the reproductions into the rest of the room.

Decorative detail, rather than content, determines the over-all style: straight lines are opposed to curves, rectangles to circles, to produce the maximum of contrast. In the living room, the lushly rounded and curved human figures in a Gauguin print match a similarly rounded lamp base with curved design. The straight-edged frame of the picture is paralleled by two rectangular cushions on the couch. And, for contrast: Gauguin figures are opposed to rectangular frame; rounded lamp is confronted with straight-edged cushions; and, in another part of the room, the roundness of lamp and drapery sets off the straight lines of magazines and Venetian blinds.

In the hallway, the counterpoint of angular and rounded forms is pushed to a further extreme. Four prints of identical size—two dealing with summer foliage and two with stark winter landscapes—flank the mirror above the credenza. The angularity of mirror and credenza is offset by the curved forms of crystal hurricane lamps and covered bowl. Their mirrored image makes the hurricane lamps seem to be four in number, thus matching the number of prints. The whole ensemble is multiplied in its reflection in the glass top of the credenza.

Additional pictures of House D are in the following plates: 57, Tête-à-tête at right angles, Sit down by invitation only; 59, Splendor of privacy; 61, Dumping, Piling.

Magazines in review

Animate and inanimate flora

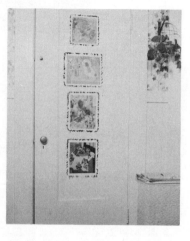

Garlands around the still life

Absolute symmetry

The systematic ivy

HOUSE E: THE EMBELLISHED CASEMENT

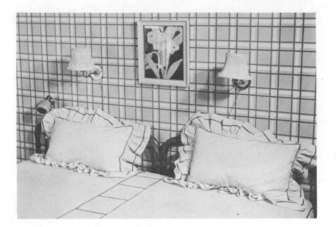

Frames everywhere   Frames within frames

THE EMBELLISHED CASEMENT: House E

The demarcation of boundaries and the emphasis upon frames give House E a unique flavor. Angular and scalloped lines encase objects and emphasize their periphery. The angular slicing of space, the avoidance of transitions, and the clustering of other objects contrast markedly with all the other houses. Objects are assembled in shadowboxes or containers; windows are framed by draperies and topped by valances, and light may be shut out by Venetian blinds. The treatment of windows parallels the angularity of the shadowboxes. The bedroom wallpaper continues the square motif; even the arrangement of the rectangular cigarette box on a square table contributes to the general theme.

Framing is only one of the methods employed to mark boundaries. Interposed membranes are also used to separate; doilies on tables and the television set divide object from surface.

Embellishment is as important as framing in this house, particularly the embellishment of the frame itself. Each frame takes on an individuality of its own through scalloping, contrasting tones, flounces, illustrations on frames or boxes, a mirror within one shadowbox, fabrics of various patterns, a feather enhancing the shadowbox that houses the china lamb. Interwoven with angularity is a decorative theme of leaves and flowers, which attenuates rigid demarcations and prevents monotony: the print of an iris on the bedroom wall; a plant design in the upholstery of the chairs and in the patterns of the rug and draperies; and, in various parts of the house, flowers, plants, and a string of pine cones. Multiple frames and demarcations somehow prevent the spectator from viewing the house as a whole. His attention is directed toward the detail, and remains arrested there.

Additional pictures of House E are in the following plates: 34, Neglect of whole: displaced object; 56, Covered covers; 57, Interpersonal hurdle; 60, Dining room with bassinet; 61, Spreading; 62, The dainty telephone, The lonely volume; 65, The doily theme; 66, Shrines and altars; 67, Heads and crowns; 68, Objects on parade; 69, Memento in a showcase.

Crockery enshrined

Fanfare for a lamb

Valance as frieze

Framing the furniture

Dividing the frame

OBJECT CHOICE AND SELF-REALIZATION: House F

This house overflows with objects of art, furniture, rugs, and fabrics. Their abundance, the care and precision with which they are arranged, and the impeccable condition in which they are kept—all mark this house as a place where wealth is meant to be enjoyed.

The quality and the value of the objects seem to command formality. They are organized according to stylistic rather than practical principles. Even though objects are set apart from each other, so that each article can be properly appreciated, their profusion creates an atmosphere of abundance.

The interior of the house is organized with a high degree of situational awareness. Location of furniture—for example, the bar (Plate 60) and table and the oversized couch and cocktail table—invites guests to be gregarious. Cocktail glasses, coasters, and shakers appeal to the thirsty palate. Although objects speak for themselves, their arrangement does not encourage spontaneous use. The luster of polished surfaces inhibits people from putting their feet on the tables, and the quality of the upholstery commands consideration for chairs and couches. But as a whole, the furniture does not lack promise of comfort.

The aggregate impression conveyed by House F is that the owners have given precise and premeditated thought to the organization and decoration of their home. The results indicate accomplished self-expression through object and object arrangement.

Additional pictures of House F are in the following plates: 32, Textile; 34, Placement of objects to satisfy impression of whole; 56, You can't tell until you've tried it; 60, Bar; 65, Direct contact; 66, Shrines and altars; 69, Wealth on parade.

HOUSE   F: OBJECT CHOICE AND SELF-REALIZATION

Living room as museum

Ask permission first

A bar like a club

Ideal for entertainment

Furniture need not be drab

Formal informality

IV THE LANGUAGE OF DISTURBED INTERACTION

I believe that the process of thought might be carried on independent and apart from spoken or written language. I do not in the least doubt that if language had been denied or withheld from man, thought would have been a process more simple, more easy, and more perfect than at present.

Samuel Taylor Coleridge

15.   SOCIAL CONFLICT AND STRESS

In the course of living, new social relations are established and old ones dissolved. Thus, mutually agreed upon approaches and separations occur without imposing undue stress upon the participants. Sometimes, however, agreements cannot be reached. Even though mutual understanding may exist, partisan interests, satisfaction of bodily needs, or matters involving personal security bring about clashes that are frustrating to all concerned. Hence, it is inevitable that people who live together are bound to interfere with one another, but it must be understood that not every interpersonal conflict is the result of psychopathology on the part of the participants. Only when a **conflict** is perpetuated for its own sake, and when mutual interference has become a goal in itself, do social conflicts become abnormal. Perpetual or repeated conflicts between the same individuals are usually caused by emotional disturbances of the participants; social conflicts are sometimes even provoked to ease unbearable internal tensions. But, more often than not, social conflict increases anxiety.

An entire series of visual or auditory cues betrays the presence of social conflict to an observer. Among the most common of these cues are those indicating such disturbances of emotions as anger, fear, anxiety, shame, guilt, and depression; all these are the result of either internal psychological conflicts or interference by other people. Regardless of the cause, the manifestations of the **alarm** in themselves can be communicated to other people, and may become the source of social conflict. Indeed, no normal individual is eager for the company of depressed or anxious persons if he can possibly avoid it. Thus the nonverbal signs of alarm are the foremost cues telling others to be on guard, to apply a different yardstick to the interpretation of messages, or to undertake the necessary steps to change the situation.

The presence of conflict is, however, not detected exclusively by means of cues indicating people's alarm. Stress is often diagnosed, not by the presence, but by the **absence of certain cues** that, if they were present, would tend to reassure people. For example, we all expect certain such emotional reactions as signs of grief on the occasion of the loss of a loved one, signs of anger after an insult, and expressions of pain following an injury. If these expected reactions are not forthcoming, we are more alarmed than we would be if they were present. An angry man who is trying to pick a fight is likely to become more infuriated if his opponent remains cool and dispassionate. Similarly, icy silence in a group situation is more indicative of stress than a smooth flow of conversation. The absence of a handshake where it might normally be expected is more suggestive of hostility than even a painful poke in the ribs. The awareness of the absence of cues presupposes a familiarity with a particular situation and other similar situations. A friend can detect whether or not a couple has just been quarreling; a mother can tell whether a tussle between children is friendly or hostile; an employee is able to sense whether an employer's seeming praise is actually to be taken as an insult.

The detection of conflict and stress is thus based upon the observation of a multitude of cues. The perception of actual signs of alarm, their comparison to expected signs of alarm, the impact of the alarm upon bystanders, and the feedback of this reaction to those who were alarmed in the first place—all are functions that can be perceived by an observer and that may contribute to his evaluation of the situation. The longer he observes the events, the more accurate his assessment is likely to be. But it is not always possible for people to wait until they have fully grasped what is happening. On many occasions a **quick assessment** and an on-the-spot decision is necessary; therefore the question presents itself as to whether visual cues exist that can inform an onlooker quickly about the presence of stress or social conflict or the existence of emergencies. In answer to this question, we might point to the fact that in the animal world all creatures seem to recognize sounds and movements that indicate the presence of danger. These are obviously related to the perception of cues that are unusual and that differ from the cues indicating safety or "business as usual," as well as to the perception of stimuli that are extremely intense and those that are known to signify danger. The same applies to human beings. The cues that warn of known danger imply the knowledge of the mechanical tasks of daily life, of weapons, and of other dangers, and the ability to distinguish friends and enemies. Those situations that contain strange and unusual stimuli—particularly those that exceed the tolerance limit of the organism—are of relevance here.

Even under peaceful circumstances, however, the occasion may arise when an **emergency situation** suddenly exists. When a man drops dead at a reception, when a bathtub overflows, when a fist fight develops, or when two cars collide—the handling of any of these situations always takes precedence over any other concerns. There are those, too, who take advantage of people's reactions by faking emergency situations—fainting on the part of young ladies during the Victorian period is a classic example. On a minor scale, the reverse happens in ordinary social intercourse: a heated conference can be interrupted for lunch and a breathing spell; in combat a temporary truce may be arranged for the burial of the dead. These breaks take precedence over the fighting. But most social conflicts and emergencies are resolved in the normal course of existence, and each cultural group, family, and individual has its own ways of meeting these problems with some degree of effectiveness. The more familiar the observer is with such conditions, the more likely he will be to detect those subtle signs that make possible the early prediction of interference with goal-changing activities.

16. LANGUAGE AND PSYCHOPATHOLOGY

The symptoms under observation in psychopathology reveal themselves as disturbances of perception, evaluation, or expression. Since signals must be coded in some way, it is obvious that such disturbances must involve an individual's internal codifications, which are generally referred to as thinking and feeling, as well as his external codifications, the language used to communicate with others.

In the course of the **development of language**, the earliest forms of codification involve the human body as a means of denotation, a phenomenon that makes it possible for parents to understand in part what is happening within the child. For example, the child shows, through an erythema on his skin, where he itches. That such a statement is perhaps unintentional is not important, since it is language in the sense that it is understandable to both mother and child. At a later period of development, when the child is learning to move, such body language is supplemented by action language. In the initial stages of its development, the child makes use of both organ and action language. In organ language, the smooth muscles obviously predominate; in action language, the striped muscles. As the child develops further, the external concomitants of earlier internal codifications recede. Inner events are less and less expressed through bodily manifestations of the intestinal, respiratory, and vascular systems, or through the skin and the smooth muscles, but more and more through physical and social action. Finally, when symbolic mastery has been achieved, verbal, gestural, and other more arbitrary forms of denotation replace some of the previously employed actions.

The psychopathology of patients corresponds to these three levels of language development. In accepting the **genetic principle** as a causative factor in the determination of psychopathology, we are in fact declaring that disturbances in thinking, feeling, and acting, as revealed through verbal behavior, are closely linked to earlier nonverbal experiences. It takes almost a decade for a child to get even a rudimentary grasp and comprehension of language, and it is precisely during this period that the foundations of personality and human relations are established. It is evident, therefore, that if we want to find interaction patterns that may explain character formation and mental disease, we must look for them in the realm of events that occurred long before the child acquired mastery of verbal communication. Until recently psychiatry has neglected to explore such nonverbal patterns, partly because of the paucity of data on interaction between children and parents and between children and siblings, and partly because of a lack of a vocabulary and of conceptual schemes capable of describing what had been observed.

With adult psychotic patients, the observation of nonverbal exchanges that occurred twenty or thirty years earlier is obviously out of the question. When a patient verbalizes his memories and a psychiatrist attempts to reconstruct earlier events, the latter usually falls into a trap, since such accounts tend to emphasize those aspects of the past that lend themselves most readily to verbal treatment. These accounts consist mainly of the names of persons and places, labels of situations, stereotyped actions, and unusual events. Even in psychoanalysis, where hours are spent in tracing emotional patterns associated with cognitive imagery, similar limitations apply.

The conclusion is inescapable that verbal expression cannot adequately represent some of the nonverbal events experienced in the past. But even more impressive is the fact that verbal expression can under no circumstances represent experiences that a patient has never had. Patients themselves are well aware of this difficulty; they continue to seek experiences and nonverbal expressions in the mode in which they had little or no experience, or in which the experiences were traumatic or frustrating. The psychosomatic patient might illustrate this point.

In patients suffering from **psychosomatic disorders,** organ language predominates, with action language secondary and verbal language employed least of all. As the patient improves during therapy, the language spectrum shifts to a predominance of action language. It has been repeatedly observed that when patients can engage in physical and social action that is used as a language, former physical symptoms disappear. Finally, when this action phase has been completed, patients eventually grow to use verbal and gestural language appropriately. Perhaps a word should be said about the qualification "appropriately." Psychosomatic patients, many of whom are highly skilled at manipulating verbal symbols, have the idea that they cannot appropriately represent their feelings and thoughts in verbal terms. Consequently their manipulation of verbal symbols does not involve their emotional participation. The same is true of **psychopaths,** who, more than any other psychopathological group, use actions as a way of conveying messages to others. The psychopath feels that no manifestation of the body at rest—glandular, muscular, or speech—is really capable of conveying his feelings and thoughts.

The marks left by a lack of early appropriate and gratifying communication through actions, gestures, and objects are permanently imprinted on the movements of many schizophrenic patients. Such **schizophrenics** are characterized by angular, jerky, uncoördinated movements, carried out with uneven acceleration and deceleration and at either too slow or too fast a tempo (38). This lack of motor agility may well be the result of insufficient practice in personal nonverbal interaction during infancy. There is evidence for believing that the lack of parents' responsiveness in terms of nonverbal action leads to such underdevelopment, which is later compensated for on the patient's part by an increased perceptual sensitivity to the actions of others. The role of a nonparticipating observer is forced upon the patient, since the lack of appropriate responses to his muscular needs prevented him from learning how to relate himself to others through movement and action.

Manic-depressives represent a quite different picture. When they are not psychotic, the cycloid temperaments make ample use of analogic codifications—they are warm, interpersonal, and sometimes artistic. By and large, the cycloid temperaments have well-rounded and coördinated movements that in many ways express a closer relationship with analogic codifications and nonverbal, interpersonal communication.

Patients may sometimes shed light on their language problems through reënactment. During a psychotic episode, both manic-depressives and schizophrenics may reproduce movements that accompanied earlier emotional experiences. Sometimes a patient may suck his thumb or caress the arm of his chair in the process of recalling early memories; another may point toward imaginary persons or hold an imaginary baby. Even more informative than such movements accompanying verbal accounts are those that occur in patients at the peak of their breakdowns. The appearance of **primitive** or uncoördinated **movements** in individuals suffering from severe functional psychoses may be viewed as attempts to reëstablish the infantile system of communication through action. It is as if these patients were trying to relive, in later life, the patterns of communication that were frustrating in early childhood, with the hope that this time there would be another person who would understandingly reply in nonverbal terms. This thesis is supported by the observations of the behavior of psychotic children (153), who tend to play with their fingers, make grimaces, or assume bizarre body positions. Their movements rarely involve other people; instead, they are directed at themselves, sometimes to the point of producing serious injuries. But as therapy proceeds, interpersonal movements gradually replace the solipsistic movements, and stimulus becomes matched to response; once these children have been satisfied in nonverbal ways, they become willing to learn verbal forms of codification for purposes of entering into relationships with others. It is worth noting that all the successful communicative therapies devised for acute mental illness are based upon analogic codifications and the stimulation of the proximity receivers: music therapy, psychodrama, dancing, play therapy, occupational therapy, as well as such treatment methods as wet packs, continuous baths, and massage. Thus it becomes one of the aims of **therapy** to provide mentally sick patients with tasks that may develop their analogic codifications into a language that can be shared with others. Once language is developed, patients are more likely to be able to learn digital forms of codification and to use them for purposes of discourse.

Treatment is usually least difficult in cases in which the patient is one who expresses his innermost thoughts and feelings in verbal terms, and in which the therapist can rely chiefly upon verbal communication. But psychiatric therapies—and this includes psychoanalysis—seem to become less effective when the patient's abnormal behavior involves action or organ language, as it does with psychopathic personalities and psychosomatic patients. If the issue of therapy is essentially one of allowing the patient to mature, as in infantile personalities, then therapy may be long and drawn out but relatively simple. But if the issue is pathology in terms of language, as with schizophrenics and psychopathic patients, much greater complexities are involved. The language failure in the schizophrenic is not the result of any lack of complexity, but because words to the schizophrenic insufficiently express his thoughts and feelings. Since agreement can be reached only by means of verbal codifications and discursive language, the schizophrenic is perpetually isolated, and even the best of his analogic codifications cannot help him to correct his erroneous information. The occasionally depressed patient is in a much better position in relation to communication. He is isolated only in his periods of depression, when he depends upon idiosyncratic and analogic codifications; but when he is not depressed, he may use words with extreme skill.

The **psychotherapeutic problem** thus involves the following considerations:

In all cases of severe mental disease, the synchronization of analogic and digital codifications is deficient, in the sense that verbal means do not evoke analogic imagery; for appropriate functioning, the verbal and analogic codifications must be synchronized to some degree.

Especially during the acute phase of a psychosis, analogic ways of expression reappear; communication through verbal means is hardly possible.

Therapy during the acute phases of a psychosis must make use of analogic means to appeal to the analogic feeling and imagery of the patient; as the patient improves, the analogically codified experiences gradually become organized through the nonverbal responses of the therapist and of others.

As this change and reorganization takes place, some of the analogic imagery can be translated into verbal terms; the unilateral, nonverbal understanding on the part of the therapist in the early phases of treatment is supplemented by bilateral verbal agreements that occur in later phases of therapy.

Verbal means can be employed successfully for therapy in those cases in which synchronization between the analogic and the verbal has already been established in childhood. This is true in the psychoneuroses of the hysterical, phobic, and compulsive types.

With infantile personalities, an attempt must be made to translate the prevailing organ and action language into verbal language, and to encourage the patient to pursue the same goal.

Even after successful therapy, a preference will continue for either the analogic or the digital types of expression. Artistically gifted persons and those extremely sensitive to human interaction tend to be on the analogic side. Those interested in the sciences, mathematics, and philosophy tend toward the digital side.

17. DISTURBANCES OF MOTION AND THEIR COMMUNICATIVE EFFECTS

In the wider field of medicine, motor disorders are the particular concern of the neurologist (65). However, few if any investigators have studied the communicative effects such disorders have upon others and, through feedback, upon the patients themselves. One of the most striking disabilities that evokes immediate general response is any kind of **paralysis.** In our culture, persons with such disturbances are at once labeled as patients, especially if a wheelchair, splints, slings, crutches, or braces emphasize their physical disabilities; special rules are set up, and special privileges are granted. Almost intuitively, pedestrians yield the right of way; buses wait for longer than their customary short stops; special seats are reserved for amputees at ball games or rallies; helpful relatives supply reading material and a radio or a television set to the paralyzed person, as though to substitute sensory input for lack of motility. Whether such stimulation is always helpful may be questioned. Actually, such restriction of action is either accompanied by a heightened output in unaffected muscle groups or the sensory input is lessened to conform to the restricted output. It is a commonplace that patients who are completely immobilized can tolerate visitors, reading, and radio and television programs for only a limited period of time. In scientific terms, McCulloch and Pitts have stated that the nervous system conserves its own level of activity so that a change in output causes a change of input (98). More often than not, the paralyzed or disabled person actually has to protect himself from stimulation and helpful hands that prevent him from exercising his own resources (9).

Many diseases reflect themselves in **facial expression** (154). Subclinical, unilateral facial palsy requires particular consideration since it is not usually interpreted by lay persons as a disability. On the paralyzed side of the face, the expressive movements lag; on the non-paralyzed side, they appear as they would in a healthy person. The effect is not unlike double talk: when the paralyzed person laughs or shows his teeth, he contracts one side of his mouth, which is moved toward the healthy side as if expressing revulsion. When he wrinkles his forehead, his one-sided frown is interpreted as a sign of superciliousness. Asymmetries of the face are found not only among the neurologically disturbed. Wolff (166) says that in the normal face the left side is less expressive than the right. This observation has relevance for both healthy and sick persons, except that among the latter the discrepancies seem to be more marked.

In contrast to these peripheral nervous lesions with one-sided effects, there is, in central lesions as in general paresis, a reduction of tone of the mimetic muscles, a wiping out

76

NEUROLOGICAL DISTURBANCES OF FACIAL EXPRESSION

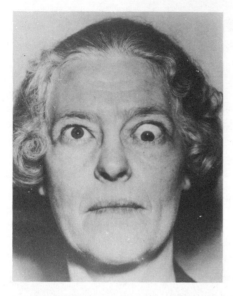

"Exophthalmic Ophthalmoplegia. Multiple palsies of the extra ocular muscles with exophthalmos and dysfunction of the thyroid." Suggesting a grim sort of humor or a desire to be perplexing.

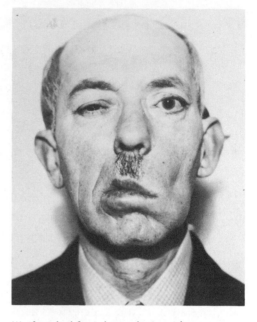

"Left-sided facial paralysis with contracture of the right facial muscles." Suggesting skepticism and revulsion.

"Ptosis due to oculomotor paralysis on the patient's right. Innervation of frontalis muscle on upward gaze." Suggesting calculated planning for an ominous scheme.

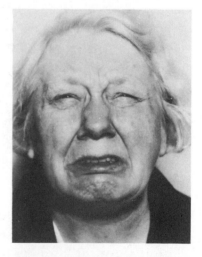

"Pathological laughing and crying. Patient with diffuse cerebral arterio sclerosis and spastic bulbar paralysis. Attacks of crying occur spontaneously, without provocation or accompanying emotion." Suggesting depression and a state of chronic annoyance.

All pictures on this plate derive from the collection of Dr. Robert Wartenberg and his *Diagnostic Tests in Neurology* and are reproduced through the courtesy of the Year Book Publishers, Inc., Chicago. Dr. Wartenberg's captions are in quotes.

of the nasolabial fold, and a loss of the finer mimetic movements. The face assumes a flabby and stupid expression, which is augmented by occasional fibrillations of the muscles. The discrepancy between a listless facial expression and the frequent grandiose verbal manifestations characteristic of the disease further increases confusion in the observer. Quite a different impression is produced by the Parkinsonian face. The palpebral fissures are usually wider than normal, and blinking is infrequent; the whole face seems immobile and greasy, and out of the half-open mouth may run a considerable amount of saliva. In ocular motor paralysis, the conjugated eye movements are likely to be disturbed, so that the two eyes do not look in the same direction. The effect upon the spectator, when he is regarded by only one eye or with neither, is an unnerving one, and likely to fill him with a sense of caution and anxiety. Especially in a culture that venerates the act of "looking somebody straight in the eye," the effect is particularly disconcerting.

Quite different impressions are conveyed by those afflicted with diseases that result in **involuntary movements.** In early written accounts, persons suffering from seizures were described as victims of a *morbus sacer* (falling sickness), and were thought to be superior beings endowed with unusual powers. In the fourteenth and fifteenth centuries, disorders characterized by motor overactivity were regarded as epidemics of dancing (St. Vitus's dance). Thus, for thousands of years, athetoid, choreatic, or tremulous movements have aroused attention, suspicion, and superstition. Tremor and intention tremor are perhaps the most significant. If someone has "the shakes," as evidenced by his grip on a glass or his actions in lighting a match or carrying out any kind of finer movements, these become signals for others to show concern.

Motor disturbances occur in functional disorders as well. For example, static ataxia— that is, the defective muscular coördination of the individual while attempting to maintain a fixed position of the body or the limbs—has been related to the presence of neuroticism (41). Retardation of movement in depressives and catalepsy in catatonics are too well known to warrant comment. Some of these disturbances are of a nature that reveals itself only when high degrees of coördination are required. Almost everyone is sensitive in some degree to precision, accuracy, rhythm, and appropriacy of movement—factors that are often subsumed under such terms as "beauty" or "charm." A girl who moves gracefully is more likely to make a favorable social impression than if she moved in a clumsy or uncoördinated way. The pleasing impression evoked by coördinated movements is in part related to the speed and rate of change of movements. A total absence of motion arouses suspicion. If someone sits on a bench for a long period without moving, the police or others are likely to investigate. Conversely, when someone moves repeatedly and agitatedly from bench to bench, he also arouses apprehension. Such examples from the cumulative body of intuitive knowledge about people and their reactions are often substantiated and heavily documented by scientists. Then too, body build and posture are closely related to bodily motion, and posture in some way reflects the actions of the muscles. **Anthropometric disproportions** not only scientifically correlate with instability of personality, lack of integration, and lessened capacity for making easy adjustments (143), but they have a communicative impact on people in social situations. The physical appearance of a dwarf, for example, not only is regarded in terms of deformity but is assumed to symbolize a fixed character structure related to a whole complex of ideas about luck and fate.

Disturbances of movement can be caused by neurological lesions in the central or peripheral portions of the efferent pathways, by lesions that affect the afferent pathways, and by lesions that affect the body image of those particular movements (140). Involuntary movements, hypertrophy and atrophy of the muscles, and spasticity are all phenomena of a gross nature and therefore are easily detectable. However, the finer disturbances of motion frequently manifest themselves only in such complex movements as **locomotion.** Morton and Fuller say: "For the phenomena of posture and locomotion, our feet are the specialized end-organs and are necessarily combined with the intervening lower limbs and the body's weight center in order that the latter be maintained in equilibrium or its desired movements be performed" (107). Hence any disturbance in the smooth performance of gait is likely to draw attention away from the face and to change the onlooker's entire attitude. Spastic gait in hemiplegia, atactic gait in tabes dorsalis, stumbling in cerebellar disorders, and hopping gait in encephalitis are well-recognized manifestations. There are those who drag their feet —especially catatonic schizophrenics—and others who practically dance when they walk— particularly manic patients. Quite aside from mental disease, everyone has characteristic patterns of walking; for example, a brisk, slinking, or hesitant gait may produce such characteristic sounds that even moods can be anticipated before a person enters a room.

If disturbances of motion are capable of being observed, their impact upon material surroundings produces traces of action that also lend themselves to interpretation. The **marks of gait** on shoes are recognized by chiropodists, neurologists, and shoemakers. Circumduction of the leg, owing to stiffness in joints or paralysis, shows up in a worn tip of the sole; spasm of the calf muscle (flexor spasm), by heavy use of the lateral edge of the sole; extensor spasm, by worn median parts of the sole; atactic gait, by the wear of the heels, with the foot brought down sharply as soldiers do on parade; stepper gait (drop foot), by wear of the sole below the balls of the feet.

Similar observations can be made regarding both gait and presence of any orthopedic deformities from footprints left in the sand or dust or on wet cement. Weakness or paralysis of one leg generally results in scraping or marks of circumduction, indicating cross-legged or scissor gait. In spastic paraplegia, the toes show deeper impressions; in atactic gait, it is the heels that show deeper impressions because of the way they are brought down. Runners space their footprints further apart than walkers. Such traces of gait are of importance to students of abnomal motion (15, 74), and to trackers, scouts, and detectives.

In **speech difficulties,** the various forms of stuttering are revealed not only by way of sound but through visual evidence of the lip and jaw movements and contraction of the neck muscles. Empathically, the onlooker may also feel embarrassment or discomfiture in the presence of people with inspiratory stridor; hyperventilation, with its shallow but rapid breathing interrupted by deep sighs, is equally alarming.

As with traces of gait, **handwriting** may reveal more than merely disturbances of motion. Ordinarily, it requires severe pathology to make handwriting totally illegible; the evidence of minor disturbances, of interest to the neurologist and the graphologist, does not give trouble to the ordinary person. Although the problem of validation of personality diagnosis by means of graphology has remained a controversial one, there is no doubt that the kinetic features observed in action are also found in handwriting: the warming-up effects in

77

AIDS TO DISTURBED LOCOMOTION

Self-propulsion

Propulsion by another

A plaster cast worn with aplomb

Crutches as subsitute for artificial limbs

Not to depend upon others
can give a sense of dignity

manics, which lead to larger characters as writing proceeds; the hypoactivity and restricted and inhibited movements in depressives (91); the punctilliousness in compulsives.

As in all cases of motor pathology, severe disturbances interfere much less with communication than do minor disturbances. If a lay person recognizes that someone is disabled, he immediately changes the communication system to comply with the cultural tradition of "being considerate." Minor disturbances, however, may escape his conscious awareness, even though he has perceived them. It is precisely in such circumstances that the greatest difficulties of communication occur. Major psychopathology is usually reflected in the movements of patients, although lay people may at first interpret their awkwardness and lack of coördination as signs of unfamiliarity with the task at hand. **Pathology of movement** and expression, however, needs to be distinguished from the movements of novices and amateurs. A person just learning a sport makes many superfluous and inept movements; indeed, learning (60) is characterized by a progressive elimination of superfluous motions. The expert, whether he is an athlete, a surgeon, or a musician, carries out his task with apparently effortless grace (64); the patient with some kind of mental pathology rarely achieves such a complete mastery, and his disturbance is relatively independent of the nature of the task.

18. DISTURBANCES OF PERCEPTION AND EVALUATION

One of the chief difficulties in studying disturbances of perception is related to the fact that experimenters must rely upon the reactions of those they study. In short, it is only the responses to perception that can be studied. However, a response necessarily presupposes evaluation and decision, so that the receptive and evaluative distinctions can scarcely be separated. Foremost among the severe disturbances of perception are those induced by pathological lesions, ranging from disorders of the sensory end organs to those of the central nervous system. The classical theory of cerebral localization, developed in the nineteenth century, assigned particular mental faculties to particular areas of the brain. At that time, a one-to-one relation was thought to exist between brain function and anatomy. Perhaps the most significant contribution of Pavlov (117) was to demonstrate how external psychological stimuli can be linked to bodily processes, thus paving the way for modern functional interpretations of anatomic patterns. According to Lashley (88), these involve perceptual patterning, the problem of stimulus equivalents, and anticipatory assumptions concerning the spread of excitation in a network of reverberatory circuits.

Recent **anatomical and physiological studies** have begun to demonstrate that analogic codifications are based upon different configurations within the organism than are digital ones. Based on clinical observation, it seems that anologic codifications involve networks that include the almost simultaneous excitation of sensory organs, the brain, and the glands and muscles. In digital codifications, the excitation of perception and effector organs seems to be much more disconnected from central functions; indeed, their functioning can be separated by long time intervals. A good example of excitation involving analogic codification is that of the very young child who can scarcely perceive, think, and react without setting his muscular apparatus in motion. It is as though the source of stimulation, the sense organs, the brain, and the muscles were connected in one large reverberatory circuit. In the adult, no such immediate connection need necessarily exist between stimulation and the organism's response, when the stimulus is of a verbal nature. In analogic codification, the signs are "felt" in the body to a much greater degree than in digital codification, where feelings of localization seem to be missing. In general, analogically perceived impressions exert a much more mandatory response than digitally perceived impressions. This is probably due to the fact that digitally or verbally codified messages need a legend for explanatory purposes, and therefore do not impinge as directly upon the organism as analogically codified messages do.

Much of the evidence concerning the difference of analogic and digital ways of codification inside the organism has been gained from the study of such disturbances as **aphasia, agnosia, and apraxia,** all of which are the result of cerebral lesions. Agnosia is a disturbance of recognition or identification. Aphasia is a disturbance that affects the memory traces of language, affecting both perception and expression. Apraxia is a disturbance that makes impossible the performance of voluntary movements, not because of paralysis but because of loss of the imagery that controls movements. Auditory verbal agnosia (word deafness), acalculia (loss of ability to calculate), agraphia (loss of ability to write), alexia (loss of ability to read), and motor aphasia (inability to speak spontaneously the words one wishes to say) are symbolic disturbances that do not affect visual, auditory, or tactile recognition of movement or objects but do affect digital and verbal recognition. Visual finger agnosia (inability to recognize the fingers by vision), tactile agnosia (loss of ability to recognize objects by touch), gustatory agnosia (loss of ability to recognize taste), olfactory agnosia (loss of ability to recognize odors), auditory musical agnosia (loss of ability to recognize music by sound) affect recognition of analogically recorded stimuli without necessarily affecting digital-verbal functions. Apraxia (inability to perform desired movement through loss of memory of how to perform it) and amimia (loss of ability to mimic gestures) constitute disturbances in the imagery of analogic language (55, 112).

These clinical pictures seem to support the theory that analogic codification, which involves phylogenetically older structures, is learned first and occupies different pathways and connections than digital and verbal codifications, which involve phylogenetically younger structures and are learned later in life. In autopsies of mentally defective children with hemiatrophy and unilateral destruction of the brain, it has been found that their histories may show no evidence of aphasic or agnostic speech difficulties (100). Apparently the centers and pathways involving speech can be localized in either hemisphere of the brain, and this localization in all likelihood is determined at the same time that the speech functions develop (14). Although at the moment psychiatrists are still unable to combine all these observations into a general theory, observations in neurophysiology and neuropathology seem to support the thesis that the fundamental differences of analogic and digital language are reflected in patterns of organization in the central nervous system, and that in all nervous and mental disorders of some severity the digital-verbal-discursive forms of language are affected earlier and more severely than the analogic-nonverbal-nondiscursive forms.

A striking clinical example illustrating this point is found in patients who have been considered deteriorated when actually their only pathology is trouble in the use of verbal and digital language to the extent that persons with agnostic, aphasic, or apraxic disturbances have been placed in institutions under the assumption that they were demented—incapable of thinking or making decisions. Every year the police apprehend persons with **"amnesia"** who later turn out to be aphasics who know who they are but are incapable of either saying or writing it. A newspaper report, published in the *San Francisco Chronicle,* October 13, 1953, illustrates this point.

> A 56-year-old Berkeley banker, missing for the last 20 months, was home yesterday after the mists of amnesia cleared and he remembered his name and address.
>
> For the whole of those 20 months, Harvey L. Morton, long-time head of the foreign exchange department of the Berkeley branch of the American

Trust Co., was in San Francisco—first as a patient at San Francisco Hospital, then at Laguna Honda Hospital.

Hospital officials here, who had cared for the ailing man, knew him only as James Foster. But it was as Harvey Morton that he wandered into his home at 2528 Chilton Way to wait in the living room until his wife came in from the garden to find him sitting there.

Still ill, partially paralyzed and hardly able to speak, Morton tried to tell his wife of the illness that robbed him of memory and the vast anonymity that had hidden him for nearly two years.

Bit by bit the story was pieced together by police on both sides of the Bay and by hospital officials after Morton's return was reported yesterday.

Morton, long a sufferer from high blood pressure, left the bank late the afternoon of February 26, 1952. He stopped at a Berkeley department store to make a small purchase and then dropped from sight. It was believed he had boarded a San Francisco-bound train, but police could not be certain.

His disappearance was reported March 3 and an all-points bulletin was issued from Sacramento immediately. It carried his full description and a record of the banker's fingerprints.

No trace could be found of the missing man. But San Francisco records show that on Feb. 27, 1952, at 7:40 P.M. a man, who signed the register as "James Foster," was found in a comatose condition in a dressing room at the Palace Baths at 85 Third street.

He was taken by ambulance to San Francisco Hospital, where his medical record shows that he was unable to speak; that there were no identifying papers or valuables in his possession and that doctors and nurses questioned his identification.

Police, both in Oakland and in San Francisco, were notified that a "James Foster or a Foster James" had been found in the bath house and the Foster record shows that no additional information about the patient could be learned at that time.

The man, known as Foster, was transferred from San Francisco Hospital to Laguna Honda Hospital on March 25, and six days later was returned to San Francisco Hospital for additional observation and treatment. Again, at this time, a check was made with police and social service files. He remained there until May 25, then went to Laguna Honda Hospital again.

San Francisco police files show that checks were made repeatedly on all "John Does" in the city's effort to trace the missing Morton. Similarly, on March 8, Berkeley police checked all San Francisco hospitals, including the county hospital, and jails and other institutions to determine whether Morton had been admitted, either under his own name or as a John Doe.

Inspector John O'Connell, head of the San Francisco Missing Persons Bureau, said that if the bureau had been notified there was a question about the identity of James Foster, the patient's prints would have been taken.

Officials at both Laguna Honda and San Francisco Hospitals said they made every effort to locate relatives of James Foster, but could find none.

Assistant Superintendent E. T. Keegan of Laguna Honda said the patient they knew as Foster was discharged from the hospital only five days ago and transferred to the ambulatory section of the home.

He was considered by them to be one of the home's permanent residents. During the 16½ months he was a patient there, the city had spent more than $3000 caring for him.

Memory returned to the banker in a flash on Sunday afternoon. Still scarcely able to speak, he walked out of his ward and downstairs. Without notifying nurses or stewards, he called a cab and went home to Berkeley, paying the driver with money he had saved from an allowance he received as a charity patient.

Mrs. Morton said she was working in the garden when some children came out to tell her a man was in the living room, waiting to see her. She went in and found her husband, whom she had almost given up for dead.

Mrs. Morton said her husband remembers only that he suffered a stroke "near a San Francisco railroad station" and that he was taken by ambulance to some hospital.

All that, she said, is unimportant now.

"At least he's home," she said, through her tears. "He's here. He recognizes us."

Morton's son, Harvey Jr., visited Laguna Honda Hospital yesterday to check his father's medical records and to make certain the James Foster who was a patient there for so long was in reality his father. The photograph was identified by a number of elderly men who were Morton's ward mates.

The **rehabilitation** of patients suffering from central lesions, including those afflicted with diffuse brain disease, is limited to those who do not suffer from diseases of a progressive nature; spectacular results have been achieved with aphasics if some functions were preserved (55). Without going into details as to the methods of rehabilitation, we can say that when the central disturbance affects both analogic and digital language, rehabilitation is out of the question. When disorientation in time and space and confusion about identity exist, the possibilities of interaction with other persons are limited. Interference with perception and evaluation makes communication almost impossible since, in the process of rehabilitation, patients rely on the assistance of others. Often it is not the severity of the brain lesion but the specific interference with communication that leads to deterioration. For example, in degenerative diseases of the aged, deterioration was traditionally blamed upon changes in the central nervous system. More recent evidence, however, indicates that the emotional and intellectual problems of senescence are in some measure related to the absence of communicative exchange. A vicious circle is established; disease results in confused perception and evaluation, which in turn restricts human interaction, thus preventing any possible correction of the confused state through communication. But if only verbal language functions are afflicted, the prognosis is much better. The evaluation of social events is based largely upon the mastery of analogic language. In a way similar to animals, most people can function without outstanding verbal gifts, as is evident in mental deficients (10). These patients can be taught to execute simple tasks and to interact with others. However, the formulation of many of these problems is only tentative. Much more work needs to be done to understand fully the implications of the importance of nonverbal and verbal language in central disturbances of the nervous system.

Peripheral disturbances of perception can be caused by lesions of the cranial and spinal nerves or the sensory end organs. Only blindness and deafness occur with sufficient frequency to be of large consequence in their impact upon society. The condition of the **blind** is particularly interesting with regard to communication. Throughout antiquity and in the Middle Ages, the blind usually led the existence of beggars; only in the second half of the eighteenth century were steps taken to educate them for useful employment. Haüy's establishment of the first school for the blind, in which embossed print was used to teach reading by touch, laid the groundwork for Braille, who, blind himself, improved upon the embossed-print system of written denotation for both speech and music (45). In a remarkable learning and relearning process, the blind person acquires the skill to substitute auditory and tactile stimuli for visual ones. If born blind, a child must wait until his motor coördination is sufficiently advanced for his fingers to explore the world of humans, animals, and objects. All three dimensional things are accessible to the blind only through tactile impressions; they naturally become experts in object language. Although the blind are capable of learning speech, they do suffer from a form of verbal unreality (32). Words used and heard do not elicit visual images; the absence of vision prevents the filling in of the numerous details that enter into the understanding of even the simplest words and concepts. The tactile image is obviously a small substitute for the visual one; touch is a proximity sensation, whereas the eye is an organ of scanning. The significance of symbols is therefore derived by the blind from their own actions rather than from the actions of others, from tactile rather than from visual scanning, and by translating events that occur in the distance into events that occur close by. Hearing, usually employed to decipher sound and speech, assumes the additional function of becoming the foremost sense for estimating distance (93). Although the blind can inform themselves about people and things by touch, they are incapable of appreciating any two-dimensional representation, either verbal or nonverbal. The blind are unique in that their development does not progress from object to picture to phonetic denotation, but instead makes an immediate jump from object to embossed phonetic denotation. Reading and writing in Braille, although alphabetical, constitutes, with its three-dimensional points in space, an object language in the truest sense of the word.

The **deaf** are usually more unfortunate than the blind, because the loss of hearing isolates them almost completely from others. An arresting example of such isolation and its consequences was reported in the *San Francisco Chronicle* on April 9, 1954. It shows how a man without means of verbal communication cannot be expected to observe the law.

The wheels of justice ground to a dead stop today in felony court— thrown out of kilter by a legal riddle never before encountered and seemingly impossible of solution.

The riddle was: How can you prosecute a man charged with felonious assault when you cannot inform him of the charges against him?

The reason for this is that the defendant cannot talk nor hear, cannot read nor write and does not know the sign language. His identification is tentative, his address is unknown and his future is uncertain.

Magistrate J. Irwin Shapiro adjourned the case until Monday and the court-assigned attorney, Benjamin Schmier, admitted he was "stumped."

The enigma presented itself in the person of a man of about 45, known as Rubin Walker. That name had been written on a card, which also said "of Alabama," when the man first strolled into the poolroom of Daniel Bramble in 1946.

Bramble said that he had employed Walker for odd jobs since then and communicated with him by showing him what to do.

Bramble told the court, however, that he had never learned where Walker lived. "He would leave when I closed and appear again next morning," he said.

Walker was arrested yesterday after witnesses said they had seen him stab Sarah Lewis, 28. Miss Lewis is now in a hospital where her condition was described as "satisfactory."

But even if she and the other witnesses testify against Walker, Schmier said, he cannot be brought to trial until a way is found to tell him of the charges.

The Sixth Amendment to the Constitution provides: "In all criminal prosecutions, the accused shall . . . be informed of the nature and cause of the accusation . . ."

Schmier pointed out that, with no means of communication, "this is impossible."

In this connection it is worth noting that historians have been puzzled by the fact that the Romans, who brought their sign and manual alphabets to such a high degree of perfection in their pantomimes, did not adapt pantomime to teaching the deaf and dumb. As far as is known, the deaf were not taught anything worth mentioning until Ponce de Leon undertook their education in Spain in the sixteenth century (34). In the seventeenth century, a number of books concerning the deaf were published and various teachers independently began to evolve methods of instruction. In the nineteenth century, education and rehabilitation of the deaf became widespread. Innumerable methods were evolved to help the deaf participate in the process of communication, a discussion of which is beyond the scope of this volume. For the communication expert, however, some of the principles evolved by Brauckmann (18) are of special interest. Since speech is produced through movement, a kinesthetic awareness of all the muscular motions involved may result in a rough understanding of spoken words. Brauckmann's method of **lip reading** teaches the deaf person to imitate the lip movements of his teacher and repeat words silently, employing all the muscles required to say a given word. When a deaf person sees another person speak, he at once begins to make the movements that have been long practiced and are familiar to him, repeating the movements necessary to make a sound. This method is fascinating because it uses visual perception of the concomitants of speech as a key to elicit kinesthetic, muscular, and other sensory sensations that can then be used to decipher statements coded in verbal terms.

19.   ART, COMMUNICATION, AND MENTAL ILLNESS

Both healthy children and mentally ill adults paint, draw, and mold forms from dirt, sand, soap, clay, and other materials, not only because they are often encouraged to do so, but because these analogic forms of codification often more closely express inner events than do words. Indeed, some of the problems of the mentally ill became apparent only when they speak or write, or when others attempt to explain in words what is wrong with them.

The interpretation of the productions of the mentally ill as a form of language is of fairly recent origin. But a deep interest in the relationship of **art and insanity** goes back as far as the Greeks, even though what they called "madness" differs considerably from current definitions. Each succeeding period in history has connected art and mental illness in varying ways. Plato believed art to emerge from a "creative delirium." Although during the Renaissance and the eighteenth century the activities of painters and poets were viewed as healthy expressions of integrated personalities, at the time of the romantic movement an approach close to that of Plato's became widespread again; at that time many thought the artist sickly. This view, which some of the poets helped particularly to encourage, was reflected in the writings of Lombroso, who set forth the notion that genius is closely related to insanity if not insanity itself (94). Max Nordau carried the line a point further, offering documentation to the effect that the artist is a degenerate (113).

It is not surprising, therefore, that in the midst of such notions connecting creative genius and insanity, a trend developed that attempted to use artistic expression for **diagnostic purposes.** In the middle of the nineteenth century a French alienist, Moreau de Tours, and his follower Max Simon laid the groundwork for the later studies of Fritz Mohr, who in 1906 worked out a series of clinical experiments to interpret the drawings of insane patients. "Mohr made his patients copy simple figures and interpreted the deviations of the copies from the original in the light of the clinical systems which were valuable for diagnostic purposes" (17). Although adaptations and refinements of such a procedure were carried on later by a number of students in Europe and America, the problem of the relationship of art and insanity was still the subject of controversy. In the early 1920's Pfeifer took the view that insane "art" is a distorted and confused version of "normal" art (119); Prinzhorn (121), who had made an extensive collection of paintings by insane patients, came to regard such works as esthetically on almost the same level as the works of sane artists.

As a more profound understanding and appreciation of the nature of primitive, abstract, and subjective art emerged the preoccupation with the relationship of art and insanity shifted away from the work of art to a concern with the psychology and personality structure of the artist or of the subject that was represented. This trend is perhaps best exemplified in Freud's "The Moses of Michelangelo" (47). In this article Freud deals with this masterpiece solely in terms of its subject matter, and is more concerned with the psychological make-up of the historical Moses than with the formal and plastic significance of Michelangelo's statue. In general, the clinical, medical, psychological, and psychoanalytic approaches to the personality of the artist leave much to be desired. Psychiatrists have rarely studied the insane artist himself; instead they have speculated about his personality after having examined his works of art. The more sensitive psychiatrists have avoided the topic altogether in the belief that art does not readily lend itself to a kind of approach that equates paintings with infantile desires and reduces the creative act to a matter of energy transformation. Those who attempt to explain the nature of art solely as the by-product of suppressions, sublimations, and substitute gratifications seem to miss the point that art is language, analogic at that, and subject to esthetic appraisal. Harry B. Lee, himself an analyst, has said: "Throughout the psychoanalytic literature about artistic sublimation, the facile ideas that the art impulse consists of transformed sexual energy and that the artist's psychic task is to deal with guilt over repressed incestuous phantasies are unquestionably accepted, repeated, paraphrased, speculated about, and romanced over, but never demonstrated." (90).

The important factor, from the **standpoint of communication,** is the meaningful impact of a work of art upon others, regardless of the state of its creator's mental health. The mental disturbances experienced by such men as van Gogh, Modigliani, Nietzsche, Hölderlin, Ruskin, Swift, and Blake, though they may color and affect their work and though our knowledge or lack of knowledge of their histories may affect what we get from their work, nevertheless do in no way diminish the cultural or communicative significance of their paintings or writings. The point of the entire issue has been succinctly expressed by Charles Lamb, who had a rather intimate acquaintance with insanity and had the additional advantage of being a highly gifted writer. The artist, he wrote, "is not possessed by his subject but has dominion over it" (87). Lionel Trilling has recently enlarged on the pertinent point: "The activity of the artist, we must remember, may be approximated by many who are themselves not artists. Thus, the expressions of many schizophrenic people have the intense appearance of creativity and an inescapable interest and significance. But they are not works of art, and although Van Gogh may have been a schizophrenic, he was in addition an artist" (158). The real artist is able to maintain the lines of demarcation between "actuality" and "fantasy." The schizophrenic is incapable of such distinctions. The whole question of schizophrenic "art" has nothing to do with distortion, obscure symbolism, repetition, or an emphasis on minute detail, which are merely external descriptive characteristics. The point is not only that the artist employs a personal style but also that he consciously shapes, selects, and refines in order to achieve an effect. Such communicative strategies as these are completely remote from the world of the schizophrenic. Works of art can be considered as a means of communication, whereas the spontaneous productions of the insane are chiefly stages of learning to communicate, and as such they have prelanguage characteristics. If it were a language, these people probably would not be patients.

In **contemporary psychiatric approaches,** the artistic expressions of the insane have been used for therapeutic purposes. Not only are the creative spells of psychotics considered part of an attempt at restitution (84) and is this creativity thought to be of a self-healing nature, but the symbolizations of the insane have been used as a basis for communicative exchange much in the same way that dreams, free association, and other verbal productions are used (109, 142). Thus in many psychiatric institutions the patients are encouraged to draw and paint, and therapists then ask for verbal comments on their work as well. The insights gained from a combination of verbal and nonverbal data are frequently of very great value, particularly when the background of the patient has been fully and carefully studied.

Modern therapeutic techniques exploit the analogic codifications inherent in all art and play (12) to establish contact with the patient, to convert artistic expression into meaningful communication, and to help the patient to translate analogically codified ideas into verbal terms. The following is an example of the correlation between a patient's painting and what he had to say about it. The **painting,** the second complete attempt by an eighteen-year-old, Turkish-born schizophrenic boy, was done after his doctor had given him water colors and gold and silver paint. It grew out of a preoccupation with his own condition, carried out in a somewhat Byzantine style remembered from his childhood and intermingled with some psychiatric notions he had learned while he was a patient. The boy was capable of talking much more freely when he explained his painting to the doctor than he could in other circumstances, and the doctor learned much about the patient that he otherwise would have missed. The patient commented:

The whole picture represents insanity, and you had better turn the picture upside-down. One side is me and my achievement in life. The picture shows the entire collapse of civilization. I am standing on a tower which is in the process of crumbling. I had [and he pointed to the fragments of the column on which he was standing] all I wanted: money, a factory, a house, an automobile. That is money in the right corner. If I were normal, I could use it as a medium of exchange. I was a member of secret societies. But the hour has come, and I put the clock in; but I have more hands on my clock because I don't know what time it is. I don't know that time exists. Evil eyes [he pointed to the stylized eyes and eyelashes] envy me, and as I tumble down I say: "Farewell to life." English language is from left to right, but I put it from right to left. As I fall down, the words are in all sorts of a mix-up. The letters are supposed to shed drops of blood amid the drop of civilization. Blood falls into the ocean with waves on top. The blood goes through these tubes to the nozzles, where they dash against the border of the painting, and then drip down in the form of icicles, and then drop down in repetition. I was sane when I did this. I am no lunatic. I have never had things like that in my mind. This skeleton is a form of insanity. My mother was twice in the psychopathic hospital. My mother's mother was insane. It is a form of heredity. Since I had seen so much of this, I had to put it on this paper. I wanted to show you nature in the raw—how a person acts and doesn't know what he is doing. An evil spirit says, "Kill and destroy," and I am condemned to an endless cycle.

The other side is reality. This person [he pointed to the figure] was once normal, put in a lunatic asylum. There are bars covering the cell. Voices are saying: "Ha ha ha, ho ho ho, hi hi hi " and show a living maniac of a huge crescendo. Took me a week to do. These spirals mean that as I was screaming, first it was low and then it went higher. There is a grave and a dagger, and a dead person floating in the river. He always thinks of destroying. Everything must be beneath the ground. He is thinking all of these things because his mind is abnormal. He is thinking that the more people he eliminated, the better he would be at heart. Green makes it more effective.

This picture is interesting and revealing, but it can hardly be considered a work of art. It does not appeal to, fascinate, or touch the onlooker except in an intellectual way. When people see the picture hanging on a wall, their curiosity is aroused; but little emotional reaction and satisfaction can be observed, except for comments on the horrors of mental disease. This reaction is probably due to the fact that although the painting represents an analogic codification, it nonetheless has numerous verbal-digital features. Letters and words appear in printed form; furthermore, the painting consists of many discrete entities, and the whole work is full of logical progressions. The sense of the analogic-continuous is missing, and the confined and fragmented is outstanding. In this sense, it represents a combined digital-verbal and analogic form of expression of the patient—a message, as it were, to the doctor, and a plea for understanding. Perhaps this picture does in some way document the language difficulties of schizophrenic patients and the function that "artistic" productions assume in the communication of these patients with the outside world.

78

PAINTING BY A SCHIZOPHRENIC PATIENT

v SUMMARY

20. TOWARD A THEORY OF NONVERBAL COMMUNICATION

In broad terms, nonverbal forms of codification fall into three distinct categories:

Sign language includes all those forms of codification in which words, numbers, and punctuation signs have been supplanted by gestures; these vary from the "monosyllabic" gesture of the hitchhiker to such complete systems as the language of the deaf.

Action language embraces all movements that are not used exclusively as signals. Such acts as walking and drinking, for example, have a dual function: on one hand they serve personal needs, and on the other they constitute statements to those who may perceive them.

Object language comprises all intentional and nonintentional display of material things, such as implements, machines, art objects, architectural structures, and—last but not least—the human body and whatever clothes or covers it. The embodiment of letters as they occur in books and on signs has a material substance, and this aspect of words also has to be considered as object language.

Analogic, nonverbal forms of codification stand in a somewhat complementary relationship to digital or verbal forms of denotation, particularly in **spatial and temporal characteristics.** Sign, action, and object languages usually require a certain space that ordinarily cannot be modified. This is not true of spoken and written languages, whose spatial requirements are minimal. For example, print can be modified in size, and microfilming makes it possible to reduce an entire library to a fraction of the space occupied by the original material. The distinctions in terms of the temporal characteristics are even more impressive. In order to be understood, words must be read or heard one after another. In written communication, the amount of time that elapses between the act of writing and the act of reading may be considerable; since a piece of writing may be composed over a long period of time and may not be read or come to light until years afterward. In contrast, the appreciation of objects and gestures is based less upon impressions that follow each other in serial order but more upon multiple sensory impressions that may impinge simultaneously.

Verbal and nonverbal languages do not appeal to the same **sensory modalities.** Silently executed sign language is perceived exclusively by the eye, much in the way that spoken language is perceived by the ear. Action language may be perceived by the eye and the ear and—to a lesser degree—through the senses of touch, temperature, pain, and vibration.

Object language appeals to both distance and closeness receivers, including the senses of smell and taste. This fact has notable effects upon the mutual position of the participants in a communication network. In practice, sign and action languages depend upon immediacy, requiring the participants to be within the range of each other's vision. Object language requires various kinds of perception, usually at a much closer range, but transmitter and perceiver need not be within reach. As a matter of fact, the transmitter may be dead when the receiver obtains the object and the message that is coded therein. In this respect, object language closely resembles written language, except that it is more universally understood.

The **selection** of a particular type **of codification** depends upon the communicative versatility of an individual and his ability to vary statements in keeping with the nature of a situation. The use of object language is indicated, for example, because of its succinct and immediate nature, in situations where a person needs to make statements to himself—he may tie a knot in his handkerchief to remind himself of something important. Action language is indicated when people wish to convey the exact nature of a situation to others; for example, certain concepts are involved in the performance of music and in the servicing of machinery—in brief, the transmission of skills—that can be conveyed only nonverbally. Verbal language is most adapted to dissecting aspects of events and to codifying such knowledge in spoken or written terms, and to carrying on meaningful discourse.

Nonverbal languages take on prime importance in situations **where words fail completely.** Words are particularly inadequate when the quality of space has to be symbolized. Photographs, paintings, drawings, material samples, or small-scale, three-dimensional models are indispensable to an appreciation of the distinctions between a Gothic cathedral and its baroque counterpart. Analogic forms of representation are equally necessary in the reporting of extreme situations, when emotional experiences are difficult to convey to those who did not personally participate in them. In an effort to suggest the quality of such events, a speaker or a writer attempts to use verbal signals that are designed to evoke emotions similar to those he or others experienced. If the listener or reader has never been exposed to or is not familiar, either through reading or other experience, with situations similar to or evocative of those described, the account will fail altogether. However, with the aid of objects and pictures, or through reënactment, even the least imaginative can be given some sense of what happened. Such verbally oriented specialists as lawyers are aware of the necessity of supplementing their verbal arguments with courtroom reënactments and of documenting them with material and pictorial evidence.

The characteristic functions of each of the various types of nonverbal language are not necessarily interchangeable. **Object language,** because of its time-enduring qualities, plays an enormous role in archaeology, anthropology, and history. Until the discovery of the first written documents to come down to us, the only enduring traces we had of the remote past were those that survived in the forms of objects and buildings. Tools and weapons were known as early as the Stone Age, and the fact that material articles almost always carry either implicit or explicit instructions with them makes it possible to reconstruct events of prehistoric times, even though we lack knowledge of the verbal language of a particular period. When we observe a tool or an implement, we consciously or unconsciously connect such objects with human activities. Somehow, when an object is assessed, the missing craftsman, inventor, or operator—either the projected self or another person—is present at the rim of consciousness, vaguely outlined though not insistent, but nonetheless felt. The interpretation is made easier because of the fact that objects either refine and increase the scope of our sensory end organs or serve to extend or replace our muscles. The modern version of sensory extension is the scientific recording instrument; that of motor extension is the labor-saving machine. In very recent years, a third kind of extension has been developed: giant calculators, computing machines, and other devices vastly extend the scope of our thinking, predicting, and decision making.

Objects may be intentionally shaped **as symbols,** or they may come to be looked upon as symbols. When they are not used for sharpening perception, facilitating evaluation, or simplifying action, they may consequently stand for something else and assume functions similar to those of words, standing for individuals, animals, activities, or other objects. The decorative aspects of materials and objects are closely related to their language functions. Whereas the referential properties of objects bear upon events that, if expressed in words, would be referred to as the subject, decoration is an expression of activities that, if expressed in words, would be called the predicate.

Nonverbal language is frequently used to effect **social control.** In interpersonal situations, many ideas, concepts, and things must be stated in ways that will not be considered obtrusive or offensive. Among such considerations is the definition of boundaries. Marks of ownership, expressed by means of objects, may be found near entrances, at gateways and doors, identifying owners or residents of a certain property and indicating how they may be reached. Such marks are particularly suitable for denoting statements to whom it may concern. Objects that stand permanently in one place and can be seen at any time impose prohibitions through their impact. Some objects are addressed to particular people; appealing interpersonally, they may invite, seduce, or repel, or demand to be looked at, touched, or tried out. We all consciously look for nonverbal clues in buildings, landscapes, and interiors, for we know that these clues have something to say about the status, prestige, taste, and other values of those who own them. Such an awareness is used by architects, decorators, and owners to set the scene for social encounters.

Object language may also be called into play when persons who make unethical, immoral, slanderous, or **profane statements** wish to hide their identity. Object language is ideal for such purposes, since it is less rigidly governed by rules than are actions or words; frequently, too, such messages are difficult to track down to their source. Thus, where words might be considered to be in bad taste or in violation of the law, many of the subtleties touching on social discrimination, emotional expression, and selective appeal are entrusted either completely or in part to nonverbal codifications.

Although verbal language often necessitates uneconomical denotation, object language allows concise and **economic phrasing.** Abbreviated statements are frequently expressed through a mixture of verbal and nonverbal language that in turn necessitates a particular kind of grammar. For example, the subject may be denoted by a three-dimensional object, whereas the predicate may be expressed in words. Here, the object identifies, the words qualify. Other statements may be repeated in nonverbal terms to avoid repetitions that might be considered boring. Human tolerance for redundancy in analogic language is far greater than its tolerance for redundancy in verbal language.

In contrast to object language, **action language** is transitory, although at the same time it represents the most universal kind of language. Among animals, auditory and visual perception of movements tend to set in motion other actions on the part of the perceiving animal. These actions may in turn influence the animal who gave the first signal. This is true of human behavior as well. Since action language exerts a kinesthetic effect, often initiating abortive movements in the perceiver, the deaf, for example, depend upon this phenomenon in the interpretation of lip reading. Indeed, almost everyone attempts to "get into the act" when watching certain physical or social actions, as can be observed from the behavior of people watching parades or from the lack of reserve on the part of sports enthusiasts. This fact is apparent in any activity that depends upon the reciprocal responses of the participants. The members of a team of acrobats in action cannot signal to each other through words or objects, but instead must rely upon split-second comprehension of each other's timing. Similarly, a spectator must experience the impact of such action himself, either visually or by actual participation, to understand fully the scope and extent of the communicative aspects of such movements.

Action language is the principal way in which **emotions** are expressed. When, in the course of a deadlocked argument, a person slams his fist upon the table, this action, along with other signs of tension, is universally understood. Other participants, almost by necessity, react with avoidant, protective, or fighting reactions. By making a switch from words to action, the referential properties of language are abruptly shifted from conflict to a context in which agreement may be possible. By means of such expression, the discussants are capable of reëstablishing contact, and may either resume their verbal discussion or separate altogether. In any event, a deadlock is broken.

Closely related to action language are **sign language and gesture.** Over the course of centuries, every social group has developed systems of communication in which particular words, signs, and gestures have been assigned communicative significance. There is a kind of gesture that assumes the auxiliary role of an emphasizing, timing, and directional device— for example, a pointed finger. Another kind of gesture takes the place of verbal signs themselves, as in Indian sign language. Because such denotation systems are not bound to phonetics, they enable persons who speak different languages to communicate with each other in ways analogous to the pictographic symbolizations that cut across verbal language barriers.

The **relationship between verbal and nonverbal codifications** can be conceptualized best through the notion of metacommunication. Any message may be regarded as having two aspects: the statement proper, and the explanations pertaining to its interpretation. The nature of interpersonal communication necessitates that these coincide in time, and this can be achieved only through the use of another channel. Thus, when a statement is phrased verbally, instructions tend to be given nonverbally. The effect is similar to an arrangement of a musical composition for two instruments, where the voices in one sense move independently and in another change and supplement each other but nonetheless are integrated into an organic and functional unity.

Combinations of the verbal and the nonverbal may be employed not only to enlighten but also **to obscure the issues** involved. In politics, business, advertising—indeed in every walk of life—words may be used to conceal forthcoming actions, and contradictory expressions are consciously used to create confusion, since human communication almost always involves object, action, and word. If all the symbolic expressions of an individual refer to the same event, then the referential aspects of the statement are clear. But when action codifications contradict verbal codifications, then confusion is almost certain to result. For example, when a mother repeatedly exclaims, "Darling, you're so sweet," simultaneously pinching her child to the extent of producing black and blue marks, the child has to learn to disregard either the action or the verbal statement in order to avoid confusion.

Finally, **verbal language** is based upon entirely different principles than the nonverbal languages. In its denotative capacity a single word can refer to a general or universal aspect of a thing or event only. In order to particularize and specify, words must be combined with other words in serial order. Words enable us to express abstractions, to communicate interpolations and extrapolations, and they make possible the telescoping of far-flung aspects of events and diversified ideas into comprehensible terms. Unlike nonverbal codifications, which are analogic and continuous, verbal codifications are essentially emergent, discontinuous, and arbitrary. The versatility of words—and this includes numbers—may, however, have dangerous consequences. Words and—to a lesser degree—gestures are commonly thought to be the principal means through which messages are conveyed. Even though such a view is not substantiated by fact, it is convenient—especially for purposes of public administration and law—to assume that we live in an almost exclusively verbal world. This emphasis upon the verbal is a by-product of modern civilization, with its accelerated centralization of control, in which increasingly more people do clerical work and fewer people are engaged in productive work. One of the consequences has been the creation of a staggering variety of middlemen who traffic solely in information. Not only salesmen but even many executives seem to have become credulous of their own propaganda, a situation that is further aggravated by the fact that most of these men have rather limited contact with many of the processes they symbolically deal with or control. The danger of this remoteness from reality lies in the tendency to regard abstract principles as concrete entities, attributing body and substance to numbers and letters and confusing verbal symbols with actual events. Such a way of thinking is an almost inescapable occupational hazard of those who use words for purposes of control.

When verbal and digital symbols are not repeatedly checked against the things they purport to stand for, **distortions of signification** may develop that **nonverbal languages seldom bring about.** Since in everyday communication these shortcomings of verbal language are difficult to avoid, people often intuitively resort to the use of nonverbal, analogic language, which is more closely tied to actual events. But this is not enough. If human beings are to protect themselves against the onslaughts of modern communications machinery and the distortions of propaganda, they must ultimately learn once again to use words scrupulously and with a sense of integrity. Only by a renewal of emphasis on the individual, with all his personal and unique characteristics—and this involves to a great extent the nonverbal —can a sense of proportion and dignity be restored to human relations.

REFERENCES

1. Adams, H. Mont St. Michel and Chartres. 401 pp. Boston and New York: Houghton Mifflin, 1904.

2. Alberti, E. A handbook of acting. 205 pp. New York: Samuel French, 1933.

3. Allport, G. W., and P. Vernon. Studies in expressive movement. 269 pp. New York: Macmillan, 1933.

4. Arieti, S. Special logic of schizophrenia and other types of autistic thought. Psychiatry, 11, 325-338, 1948.

5. Aristotle. Physiognomica. Opuscula VI (edited by W. D. Ross). 1913.

6. Arnheim, R. Art and visual perception: A psychology of the creative eye. 408 pp. Berkeley and Los Angeles: University of California Press, 1954.

7. Austin, G. Chironomia; or a treatise on rhetorical delivery. 600 pp. London: T. Cadell and W. Davies, 1806.

8. Bacon, A. M. Manual of gesture. 256 pp. Chicago: S. C. Griggs, 1875.

9. Barker, R. G., B. A. Wright, L. Meyerson, and M. R. Gonick. Adjustment to physical handicap and illness: A survey of the social psychology of physique and disability. 440 pp. New York: Soc. Sci. Res. Counc. Bull. #55 (revised), 1953.

10. Benda, C. E. Developmental disorders of mentation and cerebral palsies. 565 pp. New York: Grune & Stratton, 1952.

11. Benda, W. T. Masks. 128 pp. New York: Watson-Guptill, 1944.

12. Bender, L. Child psychiatric techniques. 335 pp. Springfield, Ill., Thomas, 1952.

13. Blake, R. R., and G. V. Ramsey. Perception: An approach to personality. 442 pp. New York: Ronald Press, 1951.

14. Blau, A. The master hand. 206 pp. New York: Amer. Orthopsychiatric Assn. Res. Monog. #5. 1946.

15. Bogen, H., and O. Lipmann. Gang und Charakter. 122 pp. Leipzig: Barth, 1931.

16. Bohrad, M. G., and H. L. Gibson. Photography in medical research. Pp. 128-157 in Medical research: a symposium (A. Smith, ed.). Philadelphia: Lippincott, 1946.

17. Born, W. The art of the insane. Ciba Symposia, 7, 202-236, 1946.

18. Brauckmann, K. Die Verkehrsfähigkeit der Gehörleidenden und das Absehproblem. Jena: Fischer, 1923.

19. Breuil, H. Four hundred centuries of cave art. 413 pp. Montignac, Dordogne: Centre d'Etudes et de Documentation Préhistoriques, 1952.

20. Brewster, A. J., H. H. Palmer and R. G. Ingram. Introduction to advertising (5th ed.). 527 pp. New York: McGraw-Hill, 1947.

21. Bühler, C. The first year of life. 281 pp. New York: John Day, 1930.

22. Bühler, K. Ausdruckstheorie. 244 pp. Jena: Fischer, 1933.

23. Burke, K. A grammar of motives. 530 pp. New York: Prentice-Hall, 1945.

24. Buxbaum, E. Transference and group formation in children and adolescents. Pp. 351-365 in The psychoanalytic study of the child, vol. 1. New York: International Universities Press, 1945.

25. Cannon, W. B. Bodily changes in pain, hunger, fear, and rage. 404 pp. New York and London: Appleton, 1929.

26. Cassirer, E. An essay on man (1944). 294 pp. Garden City: Doubleday, 1953.

27. Chang Tung-Sun. A Chinese philosopher's theory of knowledge. ETC., 9, 203-226, 1952.

28. Cherry, S. T., and A. J. Cherry. Otyognomy: or, the external ear as an index to character. 151 pp. New York: Neely Co., 1900.

29. Cocteau, J. Cocteau on film: A conversation recorded by André Fraigneau. 140 pp. New York: Roy, 1954.

30. Critchley, M. The language of gesture. 128 pp. London: Arnold, 1939.

31. Cummings, E. E. Collected poems. 315 pp. New York: Harcourt, Brace, 1938.

32. Cutsforth, T. D. The blind in school and society. 263 pp. New York and London: Appleton, 1933.

33. Darwin, C. The expression of the emotions in man and animals. (1872). 372 pp. New York: Appleton, 1898.

34. DeLand, F. The story of lip-reading, its genesis and development. Rev. and completed by H. A. Montague. 232 pp. Washington: Volta Bureau, 1931.

35. Driscoll, L., and K. Toda. Chinese calligraphy. 70 pp. Chicago: University of Chicago Press, 1935.

36. Efron, D. Gesture and environment. 185 pp. New York: King's Crown Press, 1941.

37. Eliot, T. S. Hamlet. In: Selected essays. 415 pp. New York: Harcourt, Brace, 1932.

38. Enke, W. Die Psychomotorik der Konstitutionstypen. Z. f. Psychol., 36, 237-287, 1930.

39. Evans, A. J. Cretan pictographs and prae-Phoenician script. 146 pp. New York: Putnam, 1895.

40. Evans, W. American photographs. 198 pp. and 87 plates. New York: Museum of Modern Art, 1939.

41. Eysenck, H. J. Dimension of personality. 308 pp. London: Kegan Paul, Trench, Trubner, 1947.

42. Flaubert, G. Bouvard and Pécuchet. (Translated by T. W. Earp and G. W. Stonier.) 348 pp. Norfolk, Conn.: New Directions, 1954.

43. Flugel, J. C. The psychology of clothes. 257 pp. London: Hogarth, 1930.

44. Forster, E. M. A passage to India. 322 pp. New York: Harcourt, Brace, 1924.

45. French, R. S. From Homer to Keller, 298 pp. New York: American Foundation for the Blind, 1932.

46. Freud, S. Psychopathology of everyday life. 342 pp. New York: Macmillan, 1914.

47. Freud, S. The Moses of Michelangelo. Pp. 257-287 in Collected papers, vol. 4. London: Hogarth, 1946.

48. Frisch, K. von. Bees. 119 pp. Ithaca: Cornell University Press, 1950.

49. Garrison, K. C. Growth and development. 559 pp. New York: Longmans, Green, 1952.

50. Gesell, A. The first five years of life (2d ed.). 393 pp. New York: Harper, 1940.

51. Gesell, A., and C. S. Amatruda. The embryology of behavior. 208 pp. New York: Harper, 1945.

52. Gesell, A. The child from five to ten. 475 pp. New York: Harper,1946.

53. Gibson, J. J. The perception of the visual world. 240 pp. Boston: Houghton Mifflin, 1950.

54. Gilbert, K. E., and H. Kuhn. A history of esthetics. 582 pp. New York: Macmillan, 1939.

55. Goldstein, K. Language and language disturbances. 373 pp. New York: Grune & Stratton, 1948.

56. Gompertz, M. The master craftsmen; the story of the evolution of implements. 268 pp. New York. Nelson, 1933.

57. Graham, H. C. Visual perception. Pp. 868-920 in Handbook of experimental psychology. (S. S. Stevens, ed.). New York: Wiley, 1951.

58. Greenberg, C. The camera's glass eye. The Nation, 162, 294-296, 1946.

59. Grisier, O. J. How to make sign advertising pay. 166 pp. Philadelphia: David McKay, 1941.

60. Hartsow, L. D. Contrasting approaches to the analysis of skilled movements. J. gen. Psychol., 20, 263-293, 1939.

61. Hayakawa, S. I. Language in thought and action. 307 pp. New York: Harcourt, Brace, 1949.

62. Hayakawa, S. I. (Editor) Language, meaning, and maturity. 364 pp. New York: Harper, 1954.

63. Hayes, F. C. Should we have a dictionary of gestures? Southern Folklore Quarterly, 4, 239-245, 1940.

64. Herrigel, E. Zen in the art of archery, 109 pp. New York: Pantheon, 1953.

65. Herz, E., and T. J. Putnam. Motor disorders in nervous diseases. 184 pp. New York: King's Crown Press, 1946.

66. Hiler, H. From nudity to raiment. 303 pp. New York: F. Weyhe, 1929.

67. Hocart, A. M. The progress of man. 316 pp. London: Methuen, 1933.

68. Hogben, L. From cave painting to comic strip: A kaleidoscope of human communication. 288 pp. New York: Chanticleer Press, 1949.

69. Humphreys, H. N. The origin and progress of the art of writing. 176 pp. London: Ingram, Cooke, 1853.

70. Huxley, A. Brave new world (1932). 311 pp. New York: Harper, 1946.

71. H. O. No. 87. International code of signals (vol. 1: Visual and sound). Washington, D. C.: Hydrographic Office.

72. Isaacs, S. The psychological aspects of child development. Mimeographed pamphlet. 33 pp. London: Evans Brothers, 1935.

73. James, H. The sacred fount. 319 pp. New York: Scribners, 1910.

74. Jendrassik, E. Klinische Beiträge zum Studium der normalen und pathologischen Gangarten. Deutsches Arch. Klin. Med., 70, 81-132, 1901.

75. Jorio, A. di. La mimica degli antichi investigata nel gestire napolitano. Napoli: Stamperia del Fibreno, 1832.

76. Kallen, H. M. Art and freedom. 2 vols. New York: Duell, Sloan & Pearce, 1942.

77. Kees, W. Robert Motherwell. Magazine of Art, 41, 86-88, March, 1948.

78. Kees, W. Dondero and Dada. The Nation, 169, 327, 1949.

79. Kees, W. A note on climate and culture. In Painting and sculpture. Berkeley and Los Angeles: University of California Press, 1952.

80. Klages, L. Handschrift und Charakter (10th ed.). 258 pp. Leipzig· Barth, 1926.

81. Klein, A., and L. C. Thomas. Posture and physical fitness. 45 pp. Children's Bureau Publications, No. 205. Washington, 1931.

82. Koch, R. The book of signs. 104 pp. London: First Edition Club, 1926.

83. Kretschmer, E. Physique and character. 266 pp. New York: Harcourt, Brace, 1925.

84. Kris, E. Psychoanalytic explorations in art. 378 pp. New York: International Universities Press, 1952.

85. Krogman, W. M. The historical aspect of the study of human constitutional types. Ciba Symposia, 3, 1058-1065, 1941.

86. LaBarre, W. The cultural basis of emotions and gestures. J. Personality, 16, 49-68, 1947.

87. Lamb, C. Sanity of true genius. Pp. 704-707 in The works of Charles Lamb. London: Oxford, 1924.

88. Lashley, K. S. Functional interpretation of anatomic patterns. Pp. 529-547 in Patterns of organization in the central nervous system. Baltimore: Williams & Wilkins, 1952.

89. Laver, J. Taste and fashion. 271 pp. London: Harrap, 1937.

90. Lee, H. B. A theory concerning free creation in the inventive arts. Psychiatry, 3, 229-293, 1940.

91. Lewinson, T. S. Dynamic disturbances in the handwriting of psychotics. Amer. J. Psychiat., 97, 102-135, 1940.

92. Lewis, M. M. Infant speech. 335 pp. New York: Harcourt, Brace, 1936.

93. Life. They see with their ears. September 28, 1953, 57-63.

94. Lombroso, C. The man of genius. 370 pp. New York: Scribner's, 1891.

95. Lorenz, K. King Solomon's Ring. 202 pp. New York: Crowell, 1952.

96. McCarthy, D. Language development in children. Pp. 476-581 in Manual of child psychology. (L. Carmichael, ed.). New York: Wiley, 1946.

97. McCausland, E. Changing New York (Photographs by Berenice Abbott). 207 pp. New York:Dutton, 1939.

98. McCulloch, W. S., and W. Pitts. The statistical organization of nervous activity. J. Amer. Statist. Assn., 4, 91-99, 1948.

99. Madariaga, S. de. Englishmen, Frenchmen, Spaniards. 256 pp. London: Oxford, 1928.

100. Malamud, N. Personal communication.

101. Mather, F. J..Western European painting of the Renaissance. 873 pp. New York: Holt, 1939.

102. Mayo, E. The human problems of an industrial civilization (1933). 2nd ed. 194 pp. Boston: Div. of Research, Graduate School of Business Administration, Harvard University, 1946.

103. Miller, G. A. Language and communication. 298 pp. New York: McGraw-Hill, 1951.

104. Montagu, M. F. A. An introduction to physical anthropology. 325 pp. Springfield, Ill.: Thomas, 1945.

105. Morris, C. W. Signs, language, and behavior. 365 pp. New York: Prentice-Hall, 1946.

106. Morris, C. W. Science, art, and technology. Kenyon Review, 1, 409-423, 1939.

107. Morton, D. J., and D. D. Fuller. Human locomotion and body form. 285 pp. Baltimore: Williams & Wilkins, 1952.

108. Murray, M. Egyptian sculpture. 207 pp. London: Duckworth, 1930.

109. Naumberg, M. Schizophrenic art: its meaning in psychotherapy. 246 pp. New York: Grune & Stratton, 1950.

110. New York Museum ofModern Art. Photography 1839-1937. (Introduced by B. Newhall). 131 pp., 1937.

111. Nicoll, A. Masks, mimes, and miracles. 408

pp. New York: Harcourt, Brace, 1931.

112. Nielsen, J.M. Agnosia, apraxia, aphasia (2d ed.). 292 pp. New York: Hoeber, 1946.

113. Nordau, M. Degeneration. 560 pp. New York: Appleton, 1895.

114. Ogden, C. K., and I. A. Richards. The meaning of meaning. 363 pp. New York: Routledge, 1936.

115. Orwell, G. Nineteen eighty-four. 314 pp. New York: Harcourt, Brace, 1949.

116. Panofsky, E. Style and medium in the moving pictures. Transition (Paris), 26, 121-133, 1937.

117. Pavlov, I. P. Conditioned reflexes. 430 pp. London: Oxford, 1927.

118. Pei, M. The story of language. 493 pp. Philadelphia: Lippincott, 1949.

119. Pfeifer, R. A. Der Geisteskranke und sein Werk: Eine Studie über Schizophrene Kunst. Leipzig: Kröner, 1923.

120. Piaget, J. The language and thought of the child. (2d ed.). 246 pp. London: Kegan Paul, Trench, Trubner,1932.

121. Prinzhorn, H. Bildnerei der Geisteskranken. Berlin: Springer, 1922.

122. Richter, G. Sculpture and sculptors of the Greeks. 613 pp. New Haven: Yale University Press, 1930.

123. Ridenour, L. N. The role of the computer. Scientific American, 116-130, September, 1952.

124. Robb, D. M., and J. J. Garrison. Art in the Western world. 1045 pp. New York: Harper, 1942.

125. Rosen, G. The worker's hand. Ciba Symposia, 4, 1307-1318, 1942.

126. Ruesch, J., and A. R. Prestwood. Anxiety, its initiation, communication and interpersonal management. Arch. Neurol. Psychiat., 62, 527-550, 1949.

127. Ruesch, J., and G. Bateson. Communication: The social matrix of psychiatry. 314 pp. New York: Norton, 1951.

128. Ruesch, J. Synopsis of the theory of human communication. Psychiatry, 16, 215-243, 1953.

129. Ruesch, J. Psychiatry and the challenge of communication. Psychiatry, 17, 1-18, 1954.

130. Ruesch, J., G. Bateson, and W. Kees. Communication and interaction in three families. 16mm sound film. Running time, about 75 minutes. Distributed by Kinesis, Inc., San Francisco. 1952.

131. Ruesch, J., and W. Kees. Children in groups. 16mm sound film. Running time, about 25 minutes. Langley Porter Clinic, San Francisco. 1954.

132. Ruesch, J., G. Bateson, and W. Kees. A problem child before and after therapy. 16mm film. Running time, about 25 minutes. Langley Porter Clinic, San Francisco. 1955.

133. Ruesch, J., and W. Kees. Approaches and leavetakings. 16mm film. Running time, about 12 minutes. Langley Porter Clinic, San Francisco, 1955.

134. Ruesch, J., G. Bateson, and W. Kees. The child who does not speak. 16mm film. Running time, about 30 minutes. Langley Porter Clinic, San Francisco, 1955.

135. Sachs, C. World history of the dance. 469 pp. New York: Norton, 1937.

136. Sand, M. The history of the harlequinade. 2 vols. London: Martin Secker, 1915.

137. Saudek, R. Experiments with handwriting. 395 pp. London: Allen and Unwin, 1928.

138. Sayce, A. H. An elementary grammar of the Assyrian language. 129 pp. London: Samuel Bagster & Sons, 1875.

139. Schapiro, M. Nature of abstract art. Marxist Quarterly, Jan.-Mar., 1937, 77-98.

140. Schilder, P. The image and appearance of the human body. 353 pp. New York: International Universities Press, 1950.

141. Scott, G. The architecture of humanism: A study in the history of taste. (2d edition, 1924). 198 pp. Garden City: Doubleday, 1954.

142. Secheheye, M. A. Symbolic realization. 184 pp. New York: International Universities Press, 1951.

143. Seltzer, C. C. Body disproportions and dominant personality traits. Psychosom. Med., 8, 75-97, 1946.

144. Shannon, C. E., and W. Weaver. The mathematical theory of communication. 117 pp. Urbana: University of Illinois Press, 1949.

145. Sheldon, W. H. The varieties of human physique. 347 pp. New York: Harper, 1945.

146. Sheldon, W. H. Varieties of delinquent youth. 899 pp. New York: Harper, 1949.

147. Sheridan, M. Comics and their creators. (New and revised edition). 304 pp. Boston: R. T. Hale, 1944.

148. Sittl, K. Die Gebärden der Griechen und Römer. Leipzig: Teubner, 1890.

149. Stanislavsky, K. Stanislavsky on the art of the

stage. 311 pp. London: Faber and Faber, 1950.

150. Stebbins, G. Delsarte's system of expression. 507 pp. New York: Werner, 1902.

151. Still, A. Communication through the ages. 201 pp. New York: Murray Hill, 1946.

152. Sullivan, H. S. The interpersonal theory of psychiatry. 393 pp. New York: Norton, 1953.

153. Szurek, S. A. Psychiatric problems in children. Calif. Med., 72, 357-362, and 454-460, 1950.

154. Thorek, M. The face in health and disease. 781 pp. Philadelphia: Davis, 1946.

155. Tinbergen, N. Social behavior in animals. 150 pp. London: Methuen, 1953.

156. Tomkins, W. Universal Indian sign language. (4th ed.). 99 pp. San Diego: W. Tomkins, 1929.

157. Train, A. K. The story of everyday things. 428 pp. New York: Harper, 1941.

158. Trilling, L. The liberal imagination. 303 pp. New York: Viking, 1950.

159. Waugh, C. The comics. 360 pp. New York: Macmillan, 1947.

160. Wespi, H.-U. Die Geste als Ausdrucksform und ihre Beziehungen zur Rede. 171 pp. Bern: Francke, 1949.

161. West, R., L. Kennedy, and A. Carr. The rehabilitation of speech. 650 pp. New York: Harper, 1947.

162. Whorf, B. L. Collected papers on metalinguistics. 52 pp. Washington: Foreign Service Institute, Department of State, 1952.

163. Wiener, N. Cybernetics, or control and communication in the animal and the machine. 194 pp. New York: Wiley, 1948.

164. Wiener, N. The human use of human beings. 241 pp. Boston: Houghton Mifflin, 1950.

165. Wolfe, C. The hand in psychological diagnosis. 218 pp. New York: Philosophical Library, 1952.

166. Wolff, W. Experimental self analysis. Ciba Symposia, 7, 1-36, 1945.

167. Woolley, C. L. Digging up the past. 138 pp. New York: Scribner's, 1931.

168. Wright, S. Gene and organism. Amer. Naturalist, 87, 5-18, 1953.

169. Wundt, W. Völkerpsychologie. (2d edition). 4 vols. Leipzig: Engelmann, 1904.

INDEX